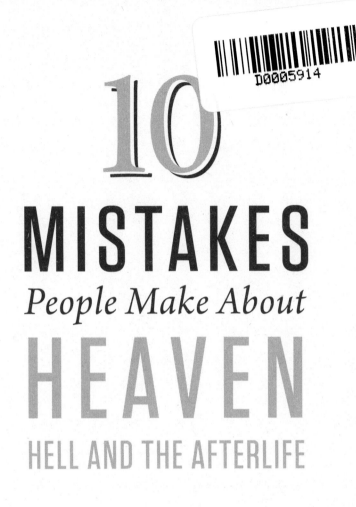

10

MISTAKES

People Make About

HEAVEN

HELL AND THE AFTERLIFE

MIKE FABAREZ

HARVEST HOUSE PUBLISHERS
EUGENE, OREGON

Cover by Brian Bobel Design, Whites Creek, TN

Cover photos © LeArchitecto / iStockphoto

10 Mistakes People Make About Heaven, Hell, and the Afterlife
Copyright © 2018 Mike Fabarez
Published by Harvest House Publishers
Eugene, Oregon 97408
www.harvesthousepublishers.com

ISBN 978-0-7369-7301-4 (pbk.)
ISBN 978-0-7369-7302-1 (eBook)

Library of Congress Cataloging-in-Publication Data is on file at the Library of Congress, Washington, DC.

Printed in the United States of America

18 19 20 21 22 23 24 25 26 / BP-SK / 10 9 8 7 6 5 4 3 2 1

Contents

What Lies Beyond the Grave?

It didn't require a thoughtful theologian to famously observe that "the statistics on death are quite impressive; one out of one people die."[1] Sadly, this is the inescapable and universal human problem. Everyone knows it. Everyone at some point feels the weight of it. And most of us, if we are honest, would love to do something to avoid its encroaching reality.

Speaking of nontheologians, it was Woody Allen, the wry comedian, who said, "I don't want to achieve immortality through my work; I want to achieve immortality through not dying."[2] But of course the odds are clearly not in his favor. He must face the prospect of his own mortality, as did his parents and grandparents, and every other generation that has ever come before him.

The dread of leaving the familiarity of this life for thought of what lies beyond led Shakespeare to pen the famous words of Hamlet's pensive soliloquy:

> To be or not to be: that is the question...To die; to sleep;
> To sleep? perchance to dream. Ay, there's the rub; For
> in that sleep of death what dreams may come when we
> have shuffled off this mortal coil, must give us pause.[3]

To say death gives the average person "pause" is to put it lightly—*panic* might be a better word. It is fair to say that people are generally fearful when forced to consider their own passing. The Bible goes so far as to say that death is the "king of terrors" (Job 18:14), to which the famous preacher Charles Spurgeon commented, "…and the terror of kings!"—which aptly reminds us that no matter who you might be, death makes no exceptions for the rich and famous.

Christianity, however, claims to have the answer to this worldwide problem. The message of Jesus, with the empty tomb as its centerpiece, is presented to a dying world. You may be tempted to think that the cross of Christ is the focal point of Christian preaching, but were you to examine the biblical record of that first generation of New Testament evangelists, you would find more time spent emphasizing Christ's resurrection from the dead, over and above any other feature of Jesus's ministry. That is not to take anything away from the profound importance of Jesus's death on the cross. Were Christ not to have suffered and died to absorb the penalty of our sinful deeds, the Bible tells us, there would be no hope for fallen people to have acceptance before God. On the other hand, to quote God's word directly: "If Christ has not been raised, your faith is futile and you are still in your sins" (1 Corinthians 15:17).

There would be no assurance, confidence, or reason to trust in the fact that Jesus's substitution for us was adequate or acceptable were it not for a verifiable victory over the grave. In other words, if the wages of sin is death (both relationally and biologically), as the Bible says, and if Jesus came to once-and-for-all deal with that sin problem by his substitutionary death, then we would rightly expect a confirmation that the death problem has been overcome as well.

You can sense the apostle Paul's elation and relief when he says that the first coming of Christ has in effect "abolished death and brought life and immortality to light through the gospel" (2 Timothy 1:10). The writer of Hebrews rejoices that the divine Jesus took on the fullness of human nature so that he might "deliver all those who through fear of death were subject to lifelong slavery" (Hebrews 2:15). For the Christian, all the sweeping effects of death—the pain, the loss, the separation—have been transformed from permanent calamities to temporary inconveniences.

> This perishable body must put on the imperishable, and this mortal body must put on immortality. When the perishable puts on the imperishable, and the mortal puts on immortality, then shall come to pass the saying that is written: "Death is swallowed up in victory." "O death, where is your victory? O death, where is your sting?" The sting of death is sin, and the power of sin is the law. But thanks be to God, who gives us the victory through our Lord Jesus Christ (1 Corinthians 15:53-57).

A SEA OF OPINION

Given the universality of the problem of death, it shouldn't surprise us that there are a variety of solutions suggested by the vast number of people longing for a remedy. Christianity lays out a logical and systematic explanation for why death exists in the first place, the manner in which God repeatedly promised to rescue us from this predicament, what exactly God did to accomplish the fix through the coming of Jesus, and how we are to go about appropriating the benefits of Christ's work. All of this is derived from data found in the Bible. And for millions of people through the centuries, this was the first place they would think to go to learn of answers to questions regarding life and death, and heaven and hell. But times are changing.

In the secularized culture of today's Western nations, the Bible is increasingly neglected as a source of truth. The problem of death remains, the quest for answers is largely unabated, but the Bible as a book that has serious answers is being cast aside. Because biblical Christianity is the only source that provides a verifiable solution to the problem of death, its information about the afterlife should be trusted. But instead, the masses of dying men and women seek insight in the philosophies and theories found in various religions, gurus, mediums, and psychics. Or perhaps in your neighborhood, workplace, or social circle your friends look to pop culture, Hollywood movies, talk shows, or hip celebrities to inform them about what lies beyond.

Either way, we can be sure that when the authoritative data found in the Bible is cast aside, the deciding factor of what is considered true ends up being everyone's own sense of what "seems right to them." If a movie script or a best-selling book resonates with one's intuition, then it is embraced as "the way things are." "This is what I believe about the afterlife" usually means "I feel like this is the way things ought to be." If we are to know with certainty what lies beyond this life, we must look to the information provided by the One who made us, initially mandated the problem in response to human rebellion, and then lovingly and graciously provided us with a way out.

GOD HAS SPOKEN

The Bible does not claim to be a book of people's best thoughts about God. Rather, it asserts that it is a precise record of God's thoughts to people. The reason we can profitably gain truth from its teaching, have our lives authoritatively corrected and redirected by its sentences, and be trained by its information to think and live as we ought, is because it claims to be God's own words.

> All Scripture is breathed out by God and profitable for teaching, for reproof, for correction, and for training in righteousness (2 Timothy 3:16).

Just as words are breathed out from a person's mouth when he speaks them, the written sentences given through the human authors of the Bible are declared to be God's very words. The Old English word translated "breathed out" was *inspired*, which came from the Latin word *inspiro,* meaning to "breathe out." Some English translations of the Bible still translate this verse from the original Greek language with the phrase "All Scripture is given by inspiration of God" (KJV, NKJV) or "All Scripture is inspired by God" (NASB, NLT, RSV). Many books written about the uniqueness of the Bible regularly utilize the phrase the "the doctrine of inspiration" to describe the fact that the Bible's data is information given to us from God.

These days, unfortunately, using the word *inspiration* in this way creates a problem. In modern English, we are accustomed to employing the word *inspiration* when we are stirred by a feeling or emotion to do something—often something creative. We might speak of what inspired an artist to paint a picture. Or what an amazing "stroke of inspiration" a musician had to write that song. Or maybe even something as mundane as "feeling inspired" to get up and clean the garage on Saturday. Because we so frequently use the word *inspiration* this way, most people think the Bible is *inspired* in the way a great novel is inspired. They would assume that what we mean is that the authors were "inspired" to write it. Or that like a thought-provoking painting, a moving book, or a rousing song, "it *is* inspiring"—as in the Bible "inspires" the person who reads it.

Those things may be true, but the claim of 2 Timothy 3:16 is that the written biblical information is as though God himself "breathed the sentences out," as someone breathes out words when speaking them to someone else. In other words, we can count on the teaching of the Bible to be profitable to accurately inform, correct, and direct our thinking on any matter it addresses because it is God's "breathed out" information. Yes, there were human authors who served as messengers of these words, but the claim is that they were conduits of God's information. That is why they are called *prophets*. The word, in the Old Testament, simply means "a mouthpiece." The picture is one of God picking up a human megaphone and speaking to the people of the world through the prophet. It is the triune God speaking by the agency of the biblical author.

In the following verses, notice the pattern of understanding the words of God's Spirit *through* the written words of the biblical authors like David or Isaiah:

> …the Scripture had to be fulfilled, which the Holy Spirit spoke beforehand by the mouth of David (Acts 1:16).

> The Holy Spirit was right in saying to your fathers through Isaiah the prophet: "Go to this people, and say…" (Acts 28:25-26).

While the God-breathed writings of David, Isaiah, Jeremiah, or Moses bear the stylistic distinctions of the human authors, the claim is that God recorded precisely what he wanted to say through these prophets in a way that preserved *his* unvarnished truth. The Holy Spirit's work over these human authors leaves us with a true and accurate written product of God's disclosed thoughts and instructions to mankind. This is much the same as when the Bible claims God's Spirit overshadowed Mary, the human mother of Jesus, so that God could bring the *living Word* into the world—arriving with the human characteristics of Mary, yet without any fallen traits or sinful deficiencies. So too the written word comes to us bearing the characteristics of the human authors, yet without deceptive data or flawed information.[4]

This claim extends beyond the Old Testament. In the New Testament, the apostles made the same assertion regarding the work of God's Spirit through them in order to declare God's truth about the work of Christ and all of its implications exactly in the way that God wanted.

> Now we have received not the spirit of the world, but the Spirit who is from God, that we might understand

> the things freely given us by God. And we impart this in
> words not taught by human wisdom but taught by the
> Spirit, interpreting spiritual truths to those who are spir-
> itual (1 Corinthians 2:12-13).

Peter equated God's message-giving work through the New Testament apostles to the same work of God's Spirit through the Old
Testament prophets (2 Peter 3:2). He went on to warn that disregarding God's messages through apostles like Paul is as perilous as
disregarding the information from God given through the Old Testament prophets (verse 16).

Any book can claim to be a record of God's words. Any person can claim to be a prophet of God or an apostle of Christ. For
that matter, anyone can claim to be God. Obviously, anyone can
claim anything. But the Bible has stood out through the centuries
as unique because it bears the expected characteristics that God is its
author. Romans chapter 1, for instance, tells us we should heed the
information in the Bible and obey its message because it is punctu-
ated by data that only God could provide—namely, a detailed set
of predictive statements that came true.

> Paul, a servant of Christ Jesus, called to be an apos-
> tle, set apart for the gospel of God, which he promised
> beforehand through his prophets in the holy Scriptures,
> concerning his Son, who was descended from David
> according to the flesh (Romans 1:1-3).

God "promised beforehand" a number of specific details "through
his prophets in the holy Scripture" that came true just as they were
recorded. This introduction doesn't afford us the space or opportunity to look at a list of these, but if you have never researched the
predictive prophecies concerning Jesus's arrival, the fate of nations,
or the forecasted chronology of various events, be sure to pick up a
book that chronicles some of these promises and their fulfillments.[5]

Just to give a sample of the kind of specificity some of these prophecies contain, consider Micah 5:2, wherein after many specific revelations regarding the details of the first coming of Christ, God's Spirit—through the agency of the prophet Micah—tells us that the everlasting Ruler of Israel was to be born in the little dusty town of Bethlehem. By itself, a promise 400 years before its fulfillment, concerning a birthplace that was statistically unlikely, may not seem overly convincing. But when you add to this the stack of other biblical prophecies that are verifiably settled centuries before they took place, you are eventually forced to concede that only the infinite and eternal God could be "declaring the end from the beginning and from ancient times things not yet done" (Isaiah 46:9-10). In the words of Wilbur Smith, the Bible

> is the only volume ever produced by man, or a group of men, in which is to be found a large body of prophecies relating to individual nations, to Israel, to all the peoples of the earth, to certain cities, and to the coming of One who was to be the Messiah. The ancient world had many different devices for determining the future, known as divination, but not in the entire gamut of Greek and Latin literature, even though they use the words prophet and prophecy, can we find any real specific prophecy of a great historic event to come in the distant future, nor any prophecy of a Savior to arise in the human race.[6]

After pointing out that the data in God's book should arrest our attention and be trusted to inform and direct our lives, Romans 1:4 points us to the verification found in Jesus's resurrection from the dead. Especially as it concerns the knowledge we are seeking about heaven, hell, and the afterlife, we should take note of the fact that the information in the Bible regarding the afterlife comes with the endorsement of an extraordinary life-after-death event. This foretold centerpiece of Christian teaching is one that is hard to believe because it defies natural law, but it is also hard to dismiss because of the manner in which it took place.

Here was a biological resurrection of the One who claimed to be here to defeat the problem of sin and death. The Old Testament had previously spoken of him living after he was slain (Isaiah 53:10-12). Jesus is recorded as speaking repeatedly about being killed and coming back to life (Matthew 16:21; 20:17-19; John 10:18). His death was a very public execution, carried out by professionals (Acts 26:22-26). His resurrection was openly attested by physical postmortem interactions with many—often many at one time (Luke 24:36-43; 1 Corinthians 15:3-7). Subsequent reports from those who testified to being eyewitnesses of a bodily resurrected Jesus refused to recant their testimony under pressure, and most ended up being executed as well.[7] Were the bodily resurrection of Christ a fabricated lie by his disciples, not only does their key assertion regarding Christianity contradict their Teacher's and their own repeated ethic for righteousness and honesty (Acts 5:3; 2 Peter 1:16), but it would seem next to impossible not to see a defector reveal the cover-up. Just as the former counsel to President Nixon during the 1972 Watergate scandal, Chuck Colson, contended about what happens when loyal conspirators are put under pressure:

> Watergate involved a conspiracy to cover up, perpetuated by the closest aides to the President of the United States—the most powerful men in America, who were intensely loyal to their president. But one of them, John Dean, turned state's evidence, that is, testified against Nixon, as he put it, "to save his own skin"—and he did so only two weeks after informing the president about what was really going on—two weeks! The real cover-up, the lie, could only be held together for two weeks, and then everybody else jumped ship in order to save themselves. Now, the fact is that all that those around the

President were facing was embarrassment, maybe prison. Nobody's life was at stake.[8]

ACCEPTING GOD'S TRUTH

All of that to say, if we are looking for trustworthy information about heaven, hell, and the afterlife, we can go to the Bible to find it. Any idea, proposal, theory, or intuitive thought can and should be weighed against the God-breathed information laid out for us in its pages. If Scripture addresses a topic clearly, the case is settled. If a suggestion about the afterlife doesn't square with the principles found in God's Word, then it has to be rejected. If the Bible doesn't give us any clue about a matter related to what lies beyond this life, then we are left to speculate, which is rarely worth our guesswork.

The Bible may not tell us everything our curious minds want to know about what lies beyond the grave, but it has given us plenty of data to dispel a ton of popular misconceptions, to keep us from believing misleading myths, and to assure our hearts when the appointment with our Maker arrives. So let us be thoughtful and discerning students of the Bible, faithful to cherish, guard, and pass on our biblical discoveries so that in the end it might be proven that in this life we were rightly informed and well prepared for the next one.

> The secret things belong to the Lord our God, but the things that are revealed belong to us and to our children forever (Deuteronomy 29:29).

CHAPTER 1

All Roads Lead to Heaven

You're at the grocery store. You're in the chip aisle. You want to buy a big bag of chips for a gathering at your house this weekend. You've got choices. Corn chips, potato chips, cheese puffs, tortilla chips, pita chips, kale chips, bean chips, lentil chips, and yes, even cricket chips. Select flat chips, chips with ridges, lattice-cut chips, or coned-shaped chips. And don't forget to choose sea salt, regular salt, no salt, or low sodium. The soda aisle is much the same—choices, choices, choices. The cornucopia of colors, flavors, sweeteners, and brands are virtually endless.

Your local supermarket carries all these options because people love their choices. One type of cheese isn't going to cut it for the clientele that frequents today's neighborhood grocery store. Imagine for a moment if you were to go to the store to buy some breakfast cereal, and all you saw in that aisle was a long row of nothing but Cocoa Puffs. Or envision the deli meat section having nothing but smokehouse barbecue bologna. I'm quite sure you would look for a new store to get your food. But if you went store-hopping and still found nothing but French onion sun chips, black cherry Fanta, Cocoa Puffs, and barbecue bologna, you would fear that you had stepped into a George Orwell nightmare. I'd venture to guess you would be willing to join the rebellion.

Surely that is how many of the people you know feel about those Bible-believing Christians who keep harping on there being only *one* way to God, only *one* true religion, only *one* true holy book, and only *one* mediator between God and man—namely, Jesus Christ. How bigoted! How intolerant! How snooty! How phobic! How narrow-minded! A quick web search for the words *narrow-minded Christians* will confirm the hostile reaction these exclusive Christian claims generate in our *open-minded,* modern culture.

EXCLUSIVITY

For all the anger and opposition expressed against the exclusive claims of Christianity—that Jesus is the only way to get right with our Creator—there is a gaping inconsistency between what people expect from a religion, compared to what they expect in several other important areas of life. Sure, they want choices when it comes to their groceries. But if they are going scuba diving, they don't want a dive shop offering them a selection of tanks—one filled with tear gas, another with a nerve agent, this one brimming with ice tea, and that one loaded with mocha almond fudge. They want a tank filled with oxygen. If they are going in for an appendectomy, they certainly don't want the nurse saying, "For your surgeon today, you have the choice of a welder, a lawyer, a waitress, or a barista." No, they want a qualified, certified, well-trained medical doctor. A first-time skydiver doesn't want to be offered the choice of a pack filled with notebooks or cell phones, Grisham novels or Band-Aids. He wants a carefully constructed and intact air-catching parachute.

It is interesting that in so many life-and-death situations, people don't want a wide variety of choices, they want the one thing that can provide what is needed. If I am suffocating, I want air, not a shopping spree. When it comes to our mortality and what lies beyond, we don't need, nor should we want, a variety of choices. What we need is the specific solution that can fix the hazard caused by a very specific problem—namely, sin!

The Bible is clear and our consciences testify that the problem we have before our Creator is sin. Humanity's moral choices, our bent for compromise and rebellion, and our engagement in a variety of sins and transgressions have put us in a situation that can be solved only by something or someone who can directly deal with the problem of sin before the tribunal of a holy God, and eradicate the dire penalty of sin. This is what Jesus said he came to do. He claimed he was uniquely qualified to do it. He said that an alliance with him, by faith, would authorize us to benefit from what he came to fix.

This is no different than having a skilled carpenter construct a lifeboat on the deck of a sinking ocean liner. As the ship begins to list and the call goes out to board the only lifeboat available, which was just graciously constructed and is now available on the starboard side of the ship, can you imagine the critic huffing about the exclusivity of this means of salvation? How foolish it would be for someone to roll his eyes and say, "There should be more ways off this sinking ship!" Or, "Why can't we just fly to safety?" Or imagine the stupidity of saying, "I might be interested in this way to get saved, if only there were an option on the port side of the ship!" If the problem is real and specific (a sinking ship), and an adequate solution has been graciously provided (a well-crafted lifeboat), then it makes no sense to neglect the means of solving the problem because there are not *more* choices!

Of course, this is what Christ claimed, and what Christianity has always preached. Our problem is sin, and the wages of sin is death. That death, as we will see, is a portal into a reality that comes with some serious consequences. But, thankfully, by his gracious provision, God sent Jesus to construct a way out of this terrible situation. There are not a lot of ways, just one. But that one well-constructed lifeboat is available and ready for you and I to climb on board.

THE SHIP IS SINKING?

Of course, the portrait painted by my little illustration will quickly be dismissed by those who think the whole dilemma couldn't possibly be real. Many think, *Come on, the ship of humanity can't possibly be sinking*, or *God wouldn't sink the ship just because we make a few mistakes*, or *This can't be, because not everyone has heard the call to get to the lifeboat*, or *This whole life-and-death scenario just seems too harsh!*

God, however, has been clear about this: The dilemma created by sin is one in which we have actively participated, and one for which we need to take responsibility. Obviously, the ship of humanity was sinking before we were born in our stateroom, in our little corner of the ship. True. There is much explained by God regarding the irreversible effects of the first guests on the ship—our great, great... great grandparents. But unlike the passengers on the Titanic, who were going about their innocent business when someone on the bridge steered them into an iceberg, when we joined the manifest on the HMS *Humanity*, we actively engaged in the subversive acts that attacked the seaworthiness of this vessel.

Within a matter of years, after being added to the passenger list, we started engaging in willful acts of sabotage. It is as though we began drilling through the hull of the ship. Every time we participated in an action that was expressly forbidden by the Commander, we were assaulting the integrity of the ship. The Captain's rules were for good. His moral laws are for the good of humanity. Every act of rebellion against God's precepts and commands are a self-destructive act of treason. Yes, our sinful words and actions are sins against our Maker, but they have a direct impact on our future well-being.

That brings me to clarify what should be obvious by now, though we are good at ignoring it: This is God's ship! It is his jurisdiction. He is the Boss, and he can make the rules. If one of my daughter's schoolteachers decreed that there would be no chewing gum in her class, well then, that's the rule. There will be consequences if my daughter breaks that rule. On her way to school in the morning the sheriff's deputies won't impose any penalties if her mouth is loaded with bubblegum. But when she steps into that classroom as a registered student in that school, she knows there will be consequences if she takes out her gum and starts chewing it. The teacher is in charge of that 1,500-square-foot teaching space, and she makes the rules.

I don't happen to like that rule. I love bubblegum. On Back to School Night I didn't give it a thought. I came in chewing away. I may have even blown a bubble for all I remember. *She's not my teacher*, I thought. *Those rules don't apply to me.* This, by the way, is how a lot of people feel about God. They think for a variety of reasons that they don't have to submit to any of the rules that they find objectionable. They may not dispute that they are in God's classroom, on God's HMS *Humanity*, but they foolishly think, *I didn't sign up for this...I will live by my own rules.*

Unfortunately, there is no way out of this one—just as at school some days my daughter feels that she didn't *sign up* for junior high either. True, I signed her up. She is a junior higher and enrolled in that third-period class whether she likes it or not. It is the same way with us. You and I are under the jurisdiction of God by birth, not by choice. Just as we didn't choose where or when to be born, we are all subject to God's rules because we are under his jurisdiction, born on his ship—which happens to be sinking because our first parents broke the rules. Every subsequent generation of passengers since has broken rules as well and has actively drilled holes in the hull of the ship.

That may not silence the objection that you would rather not be subject to something for which you never signed up, but, just like the unyielding rule that your lungs need oxygen (another law for which you and I didn't vote), there are some realities that are not democratic. The realities of sin and our need for a Savior are as fixed as our daily subjection to gravity.

THE CALL TO THE LIFEBOATS

The good news proclaimed by Christianity is that God has provided a Savior! There is a solution. Christ can rescue us from the sinking ship. There is a lifeboat that is buoyant and able to save. The exclusivity of that lifeboat is not in question in the pages of the Bible. You can't cling to the bedpost in your stateroom, no matter how sincerely, and be saved. You have to respond to the call to enter into the solution that God has graciously provided.

That call has gone out in a few different ways. At the core of what God has instilled as a testimony in each person's need is what we know of as the conscience. The Bible states that this inner voice we call *conscience* is a mechanism that has been wired by God, imprinted with his standard of right and wrong (Romans 2:15). It is said to give us the sense that something is not as it ought to be (which, by the way, isn't a bad shorthand definition of *sin*). When the first sinners did wrong in the Garden of Eden, they hid themselves out of shame and guilt (Genesis 3:8-11). They didn't need a sermon or a lecture; they knew their lives were not being lived out as they ought to have been.

Back to the ship. Our conscience can be equated to that amazing mechanism in our inner ear called the vestibular system, which impresses upon us the concern, "Hey, this ship is listing!" Our conscience sounds the alarms that everything is not well with our lives. While we are all good at justifying and rationalizing our sins, the ability of our conscience to sense the wrong that others are committing, the Bible says, is a reminder that our consciences are fine-tuned and have divinely implanted spiritual capacities that can quickly see the moral wrong throughout the sinking ship of humanity (see Romans 2:1-5 and 2 Samuel 12:1-9).

God is not only calling every human to his lifeboat of grace by their conscience, he has been making clear that this merciful provision of a lifeboat has a name—Jesus Christ. Since the first century, the call of God's commissioned preachers has shifted from

"Admit your sin problem and trust in God's merciful provision of grace" to "Admit your sin problem and trust in God's merciful provision provided in Jesus Christ!" And it is not as though this call to take responsibility for sin and trust in Christ for forgiveness has been sounding through the halls of a stable and smooth sailing boat. The ship has been listing all along, people have been sensing their need and groping for an answer to a world gone wrong, while the speakers in the hallways have been blaring for everyone to get on the lifeboat.

> The Lord himself tells us that the ultimate demonstration of his love was the provision he made for us in Christ.

The call of God's evangelists may be ridiculed and maligned by those who spurn its exclusivity, but the call to run to the only solution for our sin problem has been going out while most people are trying to do something to deal with the gnawing problem of wounded consciences, societal degeneracy, and the ravages of debauchery and evil.

LOVE'S PROVISION

It is popular these days to presume that if God loves people, then his love will win out—meaning that anyone who rejects his gracious provision of salvation in Christ would never be excluded from God's coming kingdom. But this is not the definition of the love of God described to us in the Bible. The Lord himself tells us that the ultimate demonstration of his love was the provision he made for us in Christ. The amazing love of our Creator is seen in the merciful and undeserved lifeboat! And recalling that we, as the passengers of this doomed voyage, have been actively drilling holes in the hull, and that the provision of this deliverance has come at a great personal cost to the Triune God, our sense of the Lord's love should be overwhelming. Ponder the compassionate extravagance articulated in these words:

> One will scarcely die for a righteous person—though perhaps for a good person one would dare even to die—but God shows his love for us in that while we were still sinners, Christ died for us (Romans 5:7-8).

Now that the means of our rescue has been made available, God's incredible love is expressed in the repeated warnings he provides in creation, conscience, and Christian preaching to turn to this saving provision found in Christ. God's urgent call for everyone to see their plight, admit their need, and cling to the salvation given to us in Jesus is God's ongoing expression of love. Divine love is demonstrated in the urgent declaration that salvation is needed and available in Christ. Love warns! That is what biblically minded Christians have been doing for centuries. This is the call of the first chapter of this book to any and all who presume upon the love of God—to those who may even now be persistently rejecting his means of salvation! We dare not assume that love somehow means that God will overlook our rejection of his warning. God has clearly stated that he will not. Christ is the only means of salvation! As the earliest church persistently warned:

> There is salvation in no one else, for there is no other name under heaven given among men by which we must be saved (Acts 4:12).

What was preached so clearly in the first century desperately needs to be heard in the twenty-first. Our generation must be confronted with the loving exhortation to be graciously saved from the enduring consequences our sins deserve. We must immediately get to the lifeboat!

> With many other words he bore witness and contin-
> ued to exhort them, saying, "Save yourselves from this
> crooked generation" (Acts 2:40).

AN INCLUSIVE EXCLUSIVITY

At the same time as the warning went out in Acts 2 regarding God's exclusive means of salvation, the clarification was given that this graciously provided rescue is an inclusive offer. Acts 2:39 reads, "The promise is for you and for your children and for all who are far off."

The Bible goes to great lengths to tell us that this lifeboat will be filled with many people. God's plan of salvation is a numerically big plan. It is true that not everyone will respond to God's call to repentance—actually, it will be a proportionally small response—yet we are told that through history those who by faith are saved will constitute "a great multitude that no one could number" (Revelation 7:9). As God looked down through the annals of time, he told Abraham that those who would be blessed through his redemptive plan would be like the grains of sand on the seashore, or the stars in the night sky (Genesis 15:5; 22:17; see also Galatians 3:6-9).

In those promises God gave to Abraham in the book of Genesis we also learn that God's lifeboat mission was guaranteed to be ethnically diverse. "All the nations of the earth [will] be blessed," the Lord promised (Genesis 22:18; see also 12:3). And in fact, that is how the redeemed masses are described in heaven:

> After this I looked, and behold, a great multitude that
> no one could number, from every nation, from all tribes
> and peoples and languages, standing before the throne
> and before the Lamb, clothed in white robes, with palm

branches in their hands, and crying out with a loud
voice, "Salvation belongs to our God who sits on the
throne, and to the Lamb!" (Revelation 7:9-10).

God's plan of salvation may be exclusive in terms of its means, it
might be exacting in terms of what is called for—namely, repentance
and faith—but one cannot claim it is not a big, inclusive, and diverse
plan. A widely varied and assorted selection of people have been
responding to God's call of salvation. People like Melchizedek, Jethro,
Zipporah, Rahab, Ruth, Cornelius, and a whole slew of Ninevites,
are among those who have run to get into the lifeboat before us.

Think for a minute also about the caliber of people who confess
their sins and cry out to God to be saved. Sure, there are a few who
have had impressive credentials and accomplishments, but that is
certainly not the majority. Salvation is not reserved solely for the
smart ones who can figure out the path to the lifeboat. Salvation is
not granted only to the strong ones who are sturdy enough to climb
up some steep ladder to get into the lifeboat. Seats in the graciously
provided vessel of deliverance are not granted on the basis of beauty,
brains, or brawn. Any honest observation, both inside and outside
the Bible, reminds us that this deliverance from the sinking ship of
humanity is not only numerically big and ethnically diverse, but it
is also mercifully broad.

All those who turn their noses up at the alleged exclusivity of the
Christian message of salvation would do well to rethink how inclusive this exclusive call to repentance and faith actually is. How kind,
gracious, and loving it is for God to provide such a costly salvation
to such an assorted group of undeserving sinners like us.

JESUS TALKS ABOUT ROADS

It seems everyone has an opinion about whether or not Jesus is
the only way to be saved or if instead all roads lead to heaven, so

before we leave this topic, let's make sure to let Jesus speak for himself. After all, his authoritative claims, and the proof of those claims as provided by his resurrection, uniquely qualify him to speak on the subject. Even the biggest proponents of the all-roads-lead-to-heaven view realize that this is what it comes down to (though they refuse to believe the evidence). In the introduction of a book, seeking to convince our modern generation that Jesus is not the only way, author John Hick offhandedly concedes:

> ...if Jesus was literally God incarnate, the Second Person of the Holy Trinity living a human life, so that the Christian religion was founded by God-on-earth in person, it is then very hard to escape from the traditional view that all mankind must be converted to the Christian faith.[1]

As I said in the introduction to *this* book, if the Bible is God's Book, bearing his undeniable prophetic signature, and Jesus made genuine claims to be our Savior, verifying those claims through his bodily resurrection, then it really does come down to the words of Christ in the pages of Scripture.

What do we find in his words? Absolute clarity!

After speaking about the joys and fulfillment of a future abode with God the Father that his work on the cross would secure for his disciples, he emphatically stated, "I am the way, and the truth, and the life. No one comes to the Father except through me" (John 14:6). All other roads, he plainly stated, hold no promise of forgiveness or entrance into God's favor. Elsewhere Jesus explains:

> Enter by the narrow gate. For the gate is wide and the way is easy that leads to destruction, and those who enter by it are many. For the gate is narrow and the way is hard that leads to life, and those who find it are few (Matthew 7:13-14).

The "few" Jesus speaks of here are *few* in number compared to the *large* proportion of those who reject God's gift of salvation. Throughout human history there will no doubt be a numerically large, ethnically diverse, and mercifully broad crowd who are saved, as we have seen. But tragically, there will be many more who presume upon God's love, clinging to some other false hope of acceptance before their Creator, while fighting the ongoing message of creation, their consciences, and the Christian gospel (Romans 1:16–2:16).

Surely, part of what emboldens people to assume that some road other than Christ's will be sufficient when they eventually appear before their Maker is the array of voices that continue to reinforce that idea. The "many" Jesus speaks of in Matthew 7:13-14 will include those who go around mutually affirming, "I'm okay, you're okay." "As long as we're sincere." "You'll be fine if you just try to be good." "I'm sure God will let us in."

This echo chamber of opinion may make some feel better, but every person should pause to consider whether all of this makes any sense. If God has provided Jesus for us as the means of salvation, and God is the one all of us must answer to, then surely he is in the place to construct the road that leads to salvation. He is able to provide the signage that points to its exclusive benefits, and he clearly has the rights to require us all to get on that saving highway.

HOUSE RULES

A few summers ago I took my family on a scenic drive up the California coast. Retracing one of my childhood vacations, I decided to make a stop near San Simeon at the sprawling mansion known as Hearst Castle. They still give tours of this opulent estate, just as they did when I was a kid. So, as I expected, we made our way to the visitors' center, shuffled through the line for tickets, secured our passes for the morning, boarded the bus, headed up the twisty access road through the gates, and disembarked to assemble as a group so our appointed guide could give us instructions about the tour. When he was done, we dutifully followed his lead as he ushered us through a set of massive doors leading into the first of several palatial rooms on the excursion. Our guide was careful to point out parallel red lines on the floor, which marked our path and served to remind us to stay within their boundaries as we were herded from room to room. Of course, doors that were closed were not to be entered, or even touched. Furniture behind the cordoned-off pathway was obviously off limits.

During the tour, I began to imagine what it must have been like to be William Randolph Hearst, the original resident owner of this magnificent estate—a daydream I can safely assume everyone has at some point during their visit. *How would I use this room? Would I keep the pool table here? On what occasion would I use this banquet hall?* Needless to say, these were all vain thoughts for everyone on the tour. This wasn't our house. None of us owned it. No one was going to let us move furniture, change the artwork on the wall, or jump into the pool just because we wanted to take a quick swim. We were guests, and it was interesting how everyone in my tour group knew it intuitively. We walked through the designated doors. We were careful to move into the next room only after we were invited to do so. We dutifully respected the fact that this mansion belonged to someone else.

Back in the day, the evangelistic D. James Kennedy, late pastor of Coral Ridge Presbyterian Church in Fort Lauderdale, created and popularized a pair of diagnostic questions for his evangelists-in-training. The first question directs them to ask their evangelistic prospects whether they had certainty about their entrance into heaven upon their death. The second, in essence, is a question seeking to know *why* the would-be citizen of heaven thinks he or she should be allowed in. But Dr. Kennedy strategically put this question in the mouth of God, and added a very helpful and memorable pronoun. The question reads: "Suppose that you were to die today and stand before God and He were to say to you, 'Why should I let you into my heaven?' What would you say?"[2]

"*My* heaven"!

The addition of that little pronoun *my* puts a lot of things in perspective. Whenever one raises the topic of who gets to go to heaven and how one gets qualified to live there, we would all do well to remember this is *God's* heaven we're talking about. It's not yours and it's not mine. It's his. This good place of blessing and fulfillment that people get to inhabit is his domain. He gets to set the entrance requirements. And because it is his domain, he undoubtedly has every right to determine the entrance requirements.

Just as every last person in my tour group conscientiously followed all the disclosed instructions to enter Hearst's mansion, it should not come as a surprise that we can't *wing it* when it comes to gaining access to God's mansion. The property owner has laid out the preconditions. He was very clear about them. Relying on our feelings, impressions, or intuition about what will get us in, or exclude us from *his* heaven, certainly won't cut it any more than if we were walking up to the palatial gates in San Simeon.

DECISIONS

How I respond to facts certainly won't change them. If there is a God who holds out the gracious gift of forgiveness and eternal acceptance through the only means of salvation in Jesus Christ, how we decide to react to that fact won't change the arrangement.

When the Washington State geologists sent out the warning to flee from the soon-to-erupt Mount Saint Helens in 1980, pointing all mountain inhabitants to find salvation on the road leading away from the volcanic peak, Mr. Harry Randall Truman chose to stubbornly ignore the warning. Sadly, he did so at the cost of his life.[3] The forecast was based on reliable data. The facts were the facts. The road to safety was available, but apparently the cost to pick up stakes and leave the comfortable confines of his home was too high for him. The warnings were met with a manly and confident defiance.

This is certainly the religious spirit of our age. As Henley's 1875 insolent poem against the biblically defined narrow road of Christianity declares:

> It matters not how straight the gate,
>   How charged with punishment the scroll
> I am the master of my fate,
>   I am the captain of my soul.[4]

The true and rightful Captain of our souls has provided a loving solution to the prospects of the punishment and exclusion our sins deserve. Let's listen to him. As Jesus put it two thousand years ago:

> God so loved the world, that he gave his only Son, that whoever believes in him should not perish but have eternal life (John 3:16).

CHAPTER 2

When I Die I'll Go to Sleep Until the Resurrection

What happens to us when we die? Is it anything like the corny clichés or sentimental platitudes which are so often tossed around at funerals? Is witty Brenda really up there cracking jokes with Saint Peter, or sportsman Bob getting in a round of golf on the perfectly manicured county club links of heaven? Sadly, these days people seem to be content snuggling up to their fanciful notions of what their loved one is up to. These imaginary scenes even begin to build their expectations of what lies ahead at their own death. Before we join the ranks of those who project whatever blissful scenes their imaginations can create, let us be careful to go back again to the Author of life, and govern our thoughts and hopes by what he has revealed about the reality of the afterlife.

BUT WHAT ABOUT THOSE BOOKS AND MOVIES?

It makes sense that if we want reliable information about the afterlife we ought to consult the One who conquered death for us. After all, Christ said, "I died, and behold I am alive forevermore, and I have the keys of Death and Hades" (Revelation 1:18). But what about the increasingly crowded group of experienced *experts* who make similar claims? Oh, they may not say that they are "alive forevermore," or hold any authoritative "keys" to death itself, but they certainly claim to have died and are now alive again. They also claim to have some "key information" that we don't have and probably want. Those who tell tales about life after death are very vocal about their supposed journeys to the other side, and it seems every few years there is another New York Times Best-Seller that chronicles a round-trip jaunt to heaven, hell, or somewhere in between.[1]

While some may assume that Christ's message of heaven and hell is in some way confirmed by these stories of the afterlife, the truth is, in most cases, these tales are contradictory to what God has authoritatively revealed about life after death.[2] Beyond the many unbiblical depictions of God, Christ, and heaven found in these best-sellers, the most consistent disagreement with Scripture is the portrayal of salvation as universal or nearly universal for all humanity.[3]

Having looked at this important question in the last chapter, we should be appalled that anyone would hold out the false hope that all roads (or at least most roads) lead to heaven. Or, as many would suggest, if you find yourself in the wrong place after you die, you'll have ample opportunity to get things rearranged. If in fact you can think whatever you want about Christ, believe what you would like about God, just try to be a decent person, and in the end you'll walk through that tunnel into the light to greet your grandparents, then the importance of the gospel that Jesus stressed so urgently becomes less than important.

Sensing the gravity of this misleading common thread in so many of these books and movies about the afterlife we would certainly not be alarmist to see the connection to what the Bible warns of as a kind of teaching that poses as information from an "angel of light," but is in fact satanic deception (2 Corinthians 11:14).[4] Jesus warned about those coming in his name and seeking to deceive people (Mark 13:6). He said, "False Christs and false prophets will arise and perform great signs and wonders, so as to lead astray, if possible, even the elect" (Matthew 24:24). God warned that "there will be false teachers among us" who will "bring in destructive heresies" (2 Peter 2:1). The worst destructive heresy would be to lessen the urgency or importance of the way of salvation provided exclusively in Christ.

At this point a person might say, "Well, what if everything in one of these books or testimonials lines up with what the Bible does say about the gospel and the afterlife?" Still, a few fundamental problems remain. The Bible tells us that the death experience for humans is a one-time event (Hebrews 9:27). Yes, there were a few exceptions to this in the Bible (not counting Christ), but these "resurrections" were performed in very unique circumstances to authenticate the message of Jesus or a prophet, and none of them yielded any testimonials about what we are to expect in the afterlife. The purpose of these resurrections was to point us to God's revelatory voice in the apostles and prophets about what is to come.

When the biblical authors speak of visions of heaven or proclaim the realities of hell, they are doing so as those who speak on behalf of God. The results are the "God-breathed" truths we talked about in the introduction to this book. Note what is said about these revelatory statements found on the pages of the Bible:

> ...knowing this first of all, that no prophecy of Scripture comes from someone's own interpretation. For no prophecy was ever produced by the will of man, but men spoke from God as they were carried along by the Holy Spirit (2 Peter 1:20-21).

While most of those who bring us these life-after-death testimonials want us to believe their stories, few are brazen enough to claim to be writing the eternal words of God. They want their stories to be read and their books to be purchased, but they surely don't want every word of every sentence to be held to the highest scrutiny and the ultimate authority of Scripture.

Last, it might be helpful to remember that this popular fascination with *crossing over* and coming back to report on their loved ones, quoting conversations with the deceased, and describing the experience of death is a clear violation of something God has labeled an "abomination." The Lord made clear to the settlers of the Promised Land that they were not to replicate the detestable practices of the Canaanites, who sought to cross over and return from the abode of the dead, make contact with the deceased, and inquire of those who had passed from this life to the next (Deuteronomy 18:9-12).[5]

THE BIBLICAL DATA

If we want to know what our deceased loved ones are up to or what we can expect when we die, we don't have to wait for someone to allegedly experience it and tell us about it; we can consult the God who has spoken on the topic. For curious minds like yours and mine, we might be left with a thirst for more information than God chose to disclose, but as it is with all of God's revelation, we should hang on tightly to the facts he *has* provided. As the Bible tells us,

> The secret things belong to the LORD our God, but the things that are revealed belong to us and to our children forever, that we may do all the words of this law (Deuteronomy 29:29).

The remaining chapters of this book will rely on the data God has revealed to us about the permanent residence of the saved and lost—commonly referred to as heaven and hell. This chapter, though, will seek to glean all we can from the few passages of Scripture that speak to the reality of what lies *between* this life and those two final destinies. You see, the Bible informs us that the two permanent abodes for Christians and non-Christians are not where people go *now* when they die. Two temporary places are spoken of by God, and that is why the topic of this chapter is often called "the intermediate state" by Bible teachers.

It is no wonder Christians often think wrongly about the temporary experience between this life and the eternal state—because, frankly, God didn't leave us a lot of information about it. It's not that there isn't enough revelation to correct some of the popular myths, but sadly, there will be gaps in our knowledge about this reality. Thankfully for the Christian, this is an interim residence and not our everlasting home, which is what we should rightly set our sights on.

MADE TO BE ENCASED

To zero in on an accurate expectation of the intermediate state we need to take a quick look at what the Bible teaches us about who we are as human beings. As the title of this chapter suggests, the resurrection of our bodies is the end goal. The Bible tells us that this doesn't happen right away. If I were to die today, I would leave my body behind. That may be an everyday event, but biblically speaking, that's an odd reality because that's not how we are designed to exist.

Let's go back to the beginning. When God described the creation of human beings in Genesis, he spoke of humans consisting of two component parts. One was of supreme importance because it reflected his nature and personhood—that is, our spirit. The other was a part of the fabric of the physical world that he had made, or our bodies.

> Then the LORD God formed the man of dust from the
> ground and breathed into his nostrils the breath of life,
> and the man became a living creature (Genesis 2:7).

God, of course, does not have a body; he is nonmaterial spirit (John 4:24; 1 Timothy 6:16). Each of us is also a nonmaterial spirit like God and the angels. But our spirits are also made to be encased in visible, physical matter. It is interesting to note that because sinful humans are spirits and have material bodies, Jesus, the second person of the triune God, took on a physical body to redeem us (Hebrews 10:5; Luke 24:29). As we are told:

> [Jesus] had to be made like his brothers in every respect, so that he might become a merciful and faithful high priest in the service of God, to make propitiation for the sins of the people (Hebrews 2:17).

The physical component of our humanity is so intrinsic to our nature that the word *encased* may not go quite far enough. Though we know we are able to exist without our bodies when this life is over, our spirits are so "at home" in our physical bodies that it might be more accurate to speak of our immaterial selves as being *enmeshed* in our physical containers. The entangling of a human spirit in a human body is what we generally refer to as "being alive." Humans are, as some theologians like to put it, a "psychosomatic whole"—designed to be human with both body and spirit.[6] Death, though, as the Bible describes it, is the untangling of these two components for a time, with the result that *you*—the core and essential you—is left unnaturally "naked" as it is put in the Bible (2 Corinthians 5:1-8).

DEATH

At the risk of oversimplification, we might say that at the point a person becomes a "naked human spirit," he or she has just experienced biological death. This may not be a thorough definition, but it is true, and perhaps helpful as we attempt to understand the intermediate state after we die. When a human spirit sheds his or her human body we have the biological death of that human being. Notice the following death analogy as the Bible illustrates the uselessness of claiming to trust in Christ without exhibiting any corresponding good deeds:

> For as the body apart from the spirit is dead, so also faith apart from works is dead (James 2:26).

When the body accompanies the spirit we have this current phase of life on earth. That is why the point of Jesus's death is described in this way:

> Jesus cried out again with a loud voice and yielded up his spirit (Matthew 27:50).

This description of physical death (that is, the spirit leaving the body) is not unique to Jesus. We see this same sort of description used of others way back in the book of Genesis:

> As her soul was departing (for she was dying), she called his name Ben-oni; but his father called him Benjamin (Genesis 35:18).

The same was said in the New Testament of Stephen's death when he was murdered by the angry mob.

> As they were stoning Stephen, he called out, "Lord Jesus, receive my spirit" (Acts 7:59).

Stephen's body was left under a pile of rocks, but his biological death meant that his spirit was dispatched to another place—in this instance, to be with Jesus!

For now, as you live this life, your human spirit is at home in what 2 Corinthians 5 calls a transient "tent"—your temporary "earthly home"—that is, your physical body (verse 1). But the ultimate expectation of the Christian experience is to have a better "container," described as a permanent "house" that God will reconstruct for us (verse 1). The next verse goes on to remind us that, like the apostle Paul, we should long for our eternal home—not just the permanent, physical, metropolitan place commonly called *heaven*, but the permanent, physical, bodily container often called *the resurrection body* (more on this in chapter 4). But in between these two realities is an experience this passage calls "nakedness" or "being unclothed." Notice how the following verses show not only the Christian desire to be in our permanent resurrected bodies, but also that the forthcoming disembodied state is only an interim reality, and not the goal of our longing.

> In this tent we groan, longing to put on our heavenly dwelling, if indeed by putting it on we may not be found naked. For while we are still in this tent, we groan, being burdened—not that we would be unclothed, but that we would be further clothed, so that what is mortal may be swallowed up by life (2 Corinthians 5:2-4).

While we were not originally designed to live contentedly without being encased or enmeshed in flesh, there will necessarily be a period of being "unclothed" before we receive our immortal, personal, bodily housing units. The Bible is very specific about when that takes place. As we will see later in this book, there is a promised set of future events for God's people categorized under the biblical heading "the first resurrection." For the lost there is a corresponding event we sometimes call "the second resurrection." For now, it is important to simply recognize that as human beings shed their physical bodies every day around the world in a reality we call death, there is immediately following for each one of them an intermediate state of existence that they will experience.

SLEEPING SOULS?

Some have suggested, and others have insisted, that when a person dies physically, his or her spirit enters into an unconscious state.[7]

Your "spirit goes to sleep," they say. Some teach this because they believe that the body and the soul are so inseparably bound together that we cannot have the life of the one without the other. One's conscious existence will have to wait until the resurrection of the body, they tell us. But, as we have already observed, death is described in the Bible as the successful separation of the two. The spirit lives on without the body. Stephen's spirit left his dead body and he, very much alive in spirit, began an existence in the presence of Jesus Christ—though he was "naked," or without his body.

Paul said the same when he spoke of his conflicting desires—he was torn between living on in this present world in order to serve and minister to the Philippian Christians, yet he also longed to be absent from his body and present with Christ. He expressed his dilemma in this way:

> as it is my eager expectation and hope that I will not be at all ashamed, but that with full courage now as always Christ will be honored in my body, whether by life or by death. For to me to live is Christ, and to die is gain. If I am to live in the flesh, that means fruitful labor for me. Yet which I shall choose I cannot tell. I am hard pressed between the two. My desire is to depart and be with Christ, for that is far better. But to remain in the flesh is more necessary on your account. Convinced of this, I know that I will remain and continue with you all, for your progress and joy in the faith, so that in me you may have ample cause to glory in Christ Jesus, because of my coming to you again (Philippians 1:20-26).

Before Jesus yielded up his spirit and physically died on the cross (Matthew 27:50), he told the thief who had just put his trust in him, "Truly, I say to you, today you will be with me in paradise" (Luke 23:43). Clearly, both the thief and Jesus would leave their dead bodies hanging on those horrific Roman execution crosses, yet that very day Jesus and this criminal would exist consciously and personally in another place that Jesus called "paradise" (more on that reality later). Neither of them would be spiritually unconscious or sleeping.

I have had some people who believe in sleeping souls desperately try to talk their way around this clear text of Scripture by trying to claim that if the comma is moved over one word the verse simply means that Jesus was making the point of saying those things to him "today"! In other words, "Truly, I say to you today, you will be with me in paradise." They reason, "Because the commas weren't in the original manuscripts of the Greek New Testament, then it should be assumed that this statement had nothing to do with Jesus promising that the thief would be with him in paradise that very day." Or so they say.

Not only would the word "today" make for an awkward and unnecessary person-to-person clarification, the grammar and context make it clear that Jesus was speaking of that very day.[8] The placement of the word "today" in the original Greek sentence is clear, no doubt to make a distinction in response to the penitent criminal's request, which appears in the preceding verse: "Jesus, remember me when you come into your kingdom" (verse 42). His request was focused on the future event—"when" Jesus would come into his kingdom. This future coming kingdom was the great end-times experience to which Jesus had regularly pointed people's attention (see Luke 11:2; 13:29; 14:15; 19:11; 22:16). Jesus promised this converted criminal that he would experience a blessed and satisfying personal encounter with the Christ of the kingdom that very day! This was the emphasis of Jesus's words. It was a promise that a great, sin-free, pain-free end-times reality would begin for him that very day—"today you will be with me in paradise"—even before the formal arrival of the kingdom of God on earth.

When Jesus taught us about the need to prepare for our physical death, he spoke of the moment of our death as something that separates us (our spirits) from our bodies—not in order to lie dormant and unconscious somewhere, but as very much alive, conscious, and aware of our new location. Consider the story Jesus told of the rich man and Lazarus in Luke 16.

> There was a rich man who was clothed in purple and fine linen and who feasted sumptuously every day. And at his gate was laid a poor man named Lazarus, covered with sores, who desired to be fed with what fell from the rich man's table. Moreover, even the dogs came and licked his sores. The poor man died and was carried by the angels to Abraham's side. The rich man also died and was buried, and in Hades, being in torment, he lifted up his eyes and saw Abraham far off and Lazarus at his side (verses 19-23).

Notice that when the poor Lazarus died, he was taken to a place where Abraham already was. Both the poor man and Abraham had left their bodies behind, but they—that is, their conscious spirits— were now united in a place in the afterlife. When the rich man died and his body was buried, he himself—that is, his spirit—was in a place called "Hades," leaving him with a completely different experience. This is the consistent teaching throughout the Bible. When our spirits separate from our physical bodies, we go to one of two places.

The spirits of those who will have died during the Tribulation period of the last days are described in Revelation 6 as the "souls of those who had been slain" (verse 9). These souls will not be sleeping or unconscious; rather, they will be very much aware of what is going on in heaven, and even on earth, during that crucial period of unprecedented drama upon this world. We are told that those souls will be very concerned about the injustice that is playing out, and will be asking the Lord how much longer until Christ intervenes and brings justice to the situation (verse 10).

The conscious experience of those who have already died physically is the reason we can easily understand certain statements that

Jesus made, such as the one he proclaimed to the stubborn and incredulous Jews: "Your father Abraham rejoiced that he would see my day. He saw it and was glad" (John 8:56). Abraham was not sleeping and unconscious at the incarnation of Jesus Christ, nor during his long-expected earthly ministry. He saw it play out on earth in real time, and he rejoiced. We can also understand the ease with which God could dispatch the very conscious Moses and Elijah to make a miraculous appearance on the Mount of Transfiguration with Jesus (Matthew 17:1-7). As the account tells us, these two Old Testament greats were talking with Jesus in this unique appearance, fully aware of the important unfolding earthly ministry of the Messiah.

WHAT ABOUT THOSE "SLEEPING" PASSAGES?

Much of the confusion around passages in the Bible that speak of those who have died comes from a lack of clarity regarding God's body-spirit design for humans, and our failure to appreciate God's ultimate plan for us to be encased in an eternally perfect resurrected body. If we keep these two truths in mind, we can navigate the passages that employ phrases that might otherwise lead us to the wrong conclusions.

Clarity Regarding Euphemisms

For instance, the Bible often uses euphemisms for death. A euphemism is a less jarring way to speak of something. It takes something that is very serious and puts it in less-stark terms. We use euphemisms all the time—every culture has them. And because there are few things more jarring or serious than death, every generation has sought for ways to speak more gently about this awful reality.

For example, when we speak of death today, we will often say, "Ellen has passed away," or "Jim is now at peace," or "Tina is not with us anymore," or "Steve is at rest." The Bible has its own list of euphemisms for death. In our discussion we have already encountered that Jesus "breathed his last" (Mark 15:37) or that Stephen "yielded up his spirit" (Matthew 27:50). In the Old Testament we read of David saying, "I am about to go the way of all the earth" (1 Kings 2:2) or of Abraham, who "breathed his last" and was "gathered to his people" (Genesis 25:8). But the euphemism that has led some people to believe that we are unconscious or spiritually sleeping is this: "Solomon *slept* with his fathers and was buried in the city of David" (2 Chronicles 9:31).

Imagine the words at the death of a president: "He is lying in repose in the East Room of the White House." Everyone would readily understand that this was a euphemistic way of speaking of his body. No one should think that he is literally "lying in repose"— just resting or relaxing. No, his body would be understood to be biologically dead, and, as the Bible clearly teaches, his spirit would be conscious and very much alive in one of two places. So we cannot build our understanding or expectation of the afterlife on the euphemism that appears in the Bible when it speaks of biblical characters "sleeping" in death.

Jesus utilized this common euphemism to describe the death of his friend Lazarus. When he spoke of his intention to raise Lazarus's body from the dead, his disciples misunderstood, taking this euphemism to mean he was literally sleeping, or in some kind of coma.

> He said to them, "Our friend Lazarus has fallen asleep,
> but I go to awaken him." The disciples said to him,
> "Lord, if he has fallen asleep, he will recover." Now Jesus
> had spoken of his death, but they thought that he meant
> taking rest in sleep. Then Jesus told them plainly, "Laza-
> rus has died" (John 11:11-14).

This corresponding reference to being "awakened" obviously refers to God's ultimate intention of the resurrection of the body. The Bible says that everyone will receive a resurrected body that will live on for eternity. Acts 24:15 tells us that "there will be a resurrection of both the just and the unjust." The bodies of both the saved and the unsaved will be reconstituted and made in such a way as to no longer be subject to biological death. The prophet Daniel referred to this forthcoming reality with the euphemistic images of "sleep" and "awake" when he wrote: "Many of those who sleep in the dust of the earth shall awake, some to everlasting life, and some to shame and everlasting contempt" (Daniel 12:2). To take these types of biblical statements without allowance for the euphemism, and as being inclusive of both the body and the spirit, is to ignore the rest of the clear teaching of the Bible on conscious existence after death.

Hermeneutics *and* Progressive Revelation

That's a mouthful. But these are two important terms we should know something about so that we can avoid confusion about what happens to us when we die. You'll notice that those who deny the reality of the intermediate state quote passages mostly from the early centuries of the Old Testament, and from the sections of the Old Testament that are expressing the plaintive despair of those considering their own demise.

Hermeneutics is what we call the art and science of accurately interpreting a written text. When we read the truthful statements in the Bible, we need to remember that truth will sometimes be expressed through euphemisms (as we have seen), as well as analogies, word pictures, and the faithful capturing of dialogue, which will sometimes express concepts that are not true. For instance, when Satan told Eve that if she ate from the tree she would "not surely die" (Genesis 3:4), it was a truthful depiction of what Satan said, but the words themselves were not true. The larger context of that scene, and the rest of the Bible, make that clear. Or when Peter said to Christ in Matthew 16:22 that Jesus would never suffer and die in Jerusalem, it was an accurate representation of what Peter said, but obviously the rest of the Bible shows us that the content of the statement itself was false.

This is helpful to keep in mind when reading through many of the poetic books of Scripture, which accurately express the hopelessness or raw emotions of the poets but do not reflect the truths that the rest of the Bible directs us to think or believe. Consider Job, who in his pain said, "Are not my days few? Then cease, and leave me alone, that I may find a little cheer before I go—and I shall not return—to the land of darkness and deep shadow, the land of gloom like thick darkness, like deep shadow without any order, where light is as thick darkness" (Job 10:20-22).

And in Ecclesiastes, when Solomon spoke of the hopelessness of death, he lamented, "The living know that they will die, but the dead know nothing, and they have no more reward, for the memory of them is forgotten" (Ecclesiastes 9:5), or "Whatever your hand finds to do, do it with your might, for there is no work or thought or knowledge or wisdom in Sheol, to which you are going" (verse 10). We must keep in mind the earthbound context of this "Vanity-of-vanities!-All-is-vanity!" book that the king of Israel wrote (Ecclesiastes 1:2). This is a perspective of life without God, a worldly look at how vain this existence seems to be without God or a godly perspective. But this was not the end of the story or the reality that is plainly presented to us elsewhere in the Bible.

It is also helpful to remember that God didn't hand Adam and Eve a completed Bible to read and study. Moses and his contemporaries didn't have the benefit of all that God revealed to Isaiah and Jeremiah. And in turn, Isaiah and Jeremiah lacked the fullness of the revelation God had delivered through the apostles John and Paul. We call this *progressive revelation*. It means that the further we progress in the delivery of truth—from the first written books of the Old Testament in the fifteenth century before Christ all the way to the penning of the book of Revelation near the end of the first century after Christ—the more insights people were gaining from God into a variety of important topics.

That is certainly true on the subject of the afterlife. The early narratives that accurately record people's reflections and reactions to the happenings of life and death in their day often express incomplete assumptions, which, in turn, can lead to inaccurate conclusions (for example, Job 14:10-12; Psalm 30:8-9; 88:10-12; 115:17-18). Many of these statements stem from an outlook locked on the here and now, compared to the heaven-bound value we see throughout the New Testament (Colossians 3:1-4). Observe that as the Old Testament moves forward, the direct assertions of God through his prophets and apostles pile up and fill in the truth about what we can expect after we die. Then as we read onward, the later narratives begin to depict biblical characters who reflect and react in a much more informed way.

> *When it comes to what happens to us*
> *after we die, the Bible gives us answers.*
> *Not as many as we may want, but*
> *enough for us not to be surprised.*

This simple observation illustrates another principle of wise hermeneutics: As we read Scripture, we must always distinguish between *biblical descriptions* and *biblical prescriptions*. When the Bible *describes* what someone thought, said, or did, we can certainly trust the truthfulness of the Bible that this is indeed what the person thought, said, or did. But we cannot know whether those thoughts, words, or actions are what they should be—in other words, whether or not they are actually truthful thoughts, words, or actions—unless, of course, we can point to a *biblical prescription*. A *biblical prescription* in this case is what I earlier called a "direct assertion" from God, often through the apostles and prophets (as I explained in the introduction). We always evaluate the musings and opinions of people in the narratives of Scripture by the truths plainly prescribed, stated, or held out to us in the instructive sections of God's Word.

When it comes to what happens to us after we die, the Bible gives us answers. Not as many as we may want, but enough for us not to be surprised.

HERE'S WHAT WE CAN KNOW

When you die, you will leave behind your lifeless physical body. If you are a Christian, having had your sins forgiven by Jesus, you can expect that your conscious and very-much-aware bodiless spirit will immediately be sent to be with Christ. Since the Bible tells us that Christ is in a place called heaven (more on that in chapter 4 and 5), you will be there also. That is not your permanent residence, nor will you be in your permanent condition—remember, you will be "naked" so to speak, anticipating your permanent resurrected body (more on that in chapter 4).

By contrast, if you refuse Christ and are not a Christian when you die, because your sins are not forgiven, you will not be dispatched to be with Christ. Instead, you will be sent to an unpleasant place that will house your conscious spirit until your body is resurrected. Then your life will be fairly judged and you will be assigned a permanent place, with body and spirit, in a location called "the lake of fire" (more on this dark reality in chapters 9 and 10).

While your body might lie in repose, your spirit will actively commence with either a foretaste of the reward that awaits the future residents of the New Jerusalem, or the punishment that has been promised to those who reject the gospel of Jesus Christ.

CHAPTER 3

On My Way to Heaven I'll Have to Put in Some Time in Purgatory

There are a reported 1.2 billion Roman Catholics in the world.[1] That's right—billion! I assume, like me, you have many in your life or family who identify with the Catholic Church. We love them and want them to rightly understand the truth of God's Word about heaven, hell, and the afterlife. Sadly, most of these people have gained their knowledge of these important topics from the official teaching of the Roman Catholic Church. With one in every four Americans identifying themselves as Roman Catholic, it is almost impossible to have a conversation with them about life after death without the doctrinal teachings of Rome popping up at some point in the discussion.[2] If you've ever been in such conversations, I don't have to tell you that the dominant feature of Roman Catholic teaching regarding a person's experience after death is something they call *purgatory*.

PURGATORY

The word *purgatory* comes from a Latin word which denotes a place of "purifying." It comes from a verb meaning "to purge," as in the making of something (or in this case, someone) pure, cleansed, or clean. The basic idea is that after one's death the spirits of those who will eventually be saved and brought into the presence of Christ will first need to undergo a spiritual "car wash" of sorts. But unlike a car wash, the process will be painful—really painful! The purging process will involve pain and suffering because it is a form of punishment for the sins "Christians" have committed.[3] I say "Christians" because the teaching of purgatory is not taught to be a place that determines whether or not a person will make it into heaven. It is said to be a place only for those who are saved and will definitely make it into heaven. "But as yet they are not pure and holy enough to see God, and [so] God's mercy allots them a place and a time for cleansing and preparation."[4]

This may be a very popular concept taught and believed by a billion people, but before we consider whether it is true and you should expect to experience it, we must first consider why it is so insistently affirmed as the truth.

ROMAN CATHOLIC AUTHORITY

When most people hear the words *Roman Catholic* they think *Christian*, and when people think *Christian* they think *Bible*. That makes sense, because all Roman Catholics would say they are Christians and that they look to the Bible as God's truth. But there is more to the story. Well-informed Roman Catholics will readily admit that the Bible is only one of three ways people are to discover the truth about heaven, hell, and the afterlife (and anything else that God wants us to know).

The question of how we know for sure about things we couldn't possibly know if God didn't tell us has been answered with certainty by the Roman Catholic Church throughout the centuries. We will give thought to these three sources of authority as laid out in the latest authoritative and comprehensive doctrinal statement from

Rome. It is called the *Catechism of the Catholic Church,* and it was presented to the world by Pope John Paul II in 1997. It was the most comprehensive doctrinal disclosure of Catholic teaching in almost 500 years. It seeks to articulate and clarify every significant belief and claim of the Roman Catholic Church, with the full authority of God as relayed through the Pope and the Church. Joseph Ratzinger (later to become Pope and to be known as Benedict XVI) supervised the writing of text of the *Catechism of the Catholic Church.*

The word *catechism* refers to a set of instructions used to teach students of Catholicism what the beliefs and practices of the Roman Catholic Church are and are not. That is important to remember because there may be some who say, "You can quote that *Catechism* book all you want, but I know a lot of Catholics who don't believe all those things!" When you hear that, you'll know you are listening to someone described as a "bad Catholic." The statements I will quote from the *Catechism of the Catholic Church* are the official teachings of Roman Catholicism. And the Roman Catholic Church, by its own definition, is a religion defined by its authoritative teachings as expressed most recently by the *Catechism of the Catholic Church* (*CCC*). Two successive Popes, the so-called "representatives of Christ on earth," have declared it to be so—and they claim to possess the "full, supreme, and universal power over the whole Church."[5]

So then, back to the claims of three sources of "reliable information" that should enlighten us as to what will actually happen to Christians when they die. The *CCC* states:

> It is clear therefore that, in the supremely wise arrangement of God, sacred Tradition, Sacred Scripture, and the Magisterium of the Church are so connected and associated that one of them cannot stand without the others.[6]

According to Roman Catholicism there are three avenues of accurate revelation from God to people, which are said to be so tied together that "one of them cannot stand without the other." The first is called "Tradition," which refers to what the Roman Catholic Church has practiced in its theological and devotional activities.[7] Second, Catholics are to be informed by "Sacred Scripture," the Bible.[8] And third, a source of information from God, and of most importance as we will see, is the "Magisterium." The word *Magisterium* comes from the Latin word meaning "Master." The word *Magisterium* literally means "from the Office of the Master," which they define as being from Christ himself. As they state, the Magisterium is "the living, teaching office of the Church, whose task it is to give an authentic interpretation of the word of God, whether in its written form (Sacred Scripture), or in the form of Tradition."[9] In other words, the current leadership of the Church can tell us what the Tradition of the Church and the Sacred Scripture mean.

The Roman Catholic Church is telling us here (and elsewhere) that it has the power to reveal to us important truths that we would otherwise not know were it not to disclose them to us. The Church leadership, with the Pope as its ultimate leader, can quote, explain, elaborate, and clarify the details of anything practiced in the Church (that is, Tradition) or anything written in the Bible (that is, Scripture). In the words of the *CCC*:

> In order to preserve the Church in the purity of the faith handed on by the apostles, Christ who is the Truth willed to confer on her a share in his own infallibility. By a "supernatural sense of faith" the People of God, under the guidance of the Church's living Magisterium, "unfailingly adheres to this faith."[10]

The next one is a little long, but read it carefully. It is critical to understanding how Roman Catholicism sees itself. It is quoted exactly as it appears in the *Catechism of the Catholic Church,* including all the quotation marks and the ellipsis.

> "The Roman Pontiff, head of the college of bishops,
> enjoys this infallibility in virtue of his office, when, as
> supreme pastor and teacher of all the faithful—who
> confirms his brethren in the faith—he proclaims by a
> definitive act a doctrine pertaining to faith or morals.…
> The infallibility promised to the Church is also present
> in the body of bishops when, together with Peter's suc-
> cessor, they exercise the supreme Magisterium," above all
> in an Ecumenical Council. When the Church through
> its supreme Magisterium proposes a doctrine "for belief
> as being divinely revealed," and as the teaching of Christ,
> the definitions "must be adhered to with the obedience
> of faith." This infallibility extends as far as the deposit of
> divine Revelation itself.[11]

This claim is clear. The ongoing leadership of the Roman Catholic Church can, without error, relay to us information about heaven,
hell, and the afterlife—and anything else it chooses. As the promi-
nent Catholic priest Richard John Neuhaus put it: "For the Catholic, faith in Christ and faith in the Church are one act of faith."[12]
Or as former Pope Benedict XVI stated, "The Church described as
the Incarnation of the Son continuing until the end of time."[13] The
Church and Jesus are on equal footing and are to be regarded with
equal authority.

Regarding purgatory, I learned of this claim to full authority
by the Roman Catholic Church before I read about it in Catholic literature. I was 19 years old and a fairly new Christian, visiting
some friends at the Triton College campus just outside of Chicago. I
began sharing the gospel with a student in the dining hall. We were
talking about matters of life and death, heaven and hell, and our
need for Christ and his work on the cross when, in the middle of the
conversation, four or five Catholic priests, all dressed in their black
hooded robes, sat down at the table where we were sitting. That day

I found out that Triton College was a Roman Catholic school of the Benedictine tradition. Though the college does not require their students to be Roman Catholics nor to have a belief in God, the school, as I discovered, had many devoted Catholic professors and faculty members. When the priests sat down to eat and heard my evangelistic efforts, they eventually joined the conversation.

At one point, when I was presenting the facts of the gospel and the promise of forgiveness and eternal life, one of the priests interrupted with the words: "But what about purgatory?" I'm sure I must have crinkled my brow and said something along the lines of, "And what about it? I don't have any biblical reason to believe there is a purgatory!" At that point, they all joined in with attempts to defend this well-established Catholic doctrine. Anticipating that my budding knowledge of Scripture would be put to the test, I was surprised when the Bible was never quoted. They continued to insist that "If the Catholic Church taught it, that settled it!" I assume they made reference to the Council of Florence and the Council of Trent, but in the entire discussion they never once enlisted an argument from Scripture.

I walked away that day with an education in Roman Catholicism, and how the Church understands truth. Up until that point, when I talked with "Bible believers" about heaven, hell, or the afterlife, every claim had to be evaluated by a careful reading and understanding of Bible passages. But, that day, I discovered there are a billion people who say they are Bible believers, but for them the *facts* about the afterlife are ultimately settled by what the Roman Catholic leaders have said about it.

CATHOLICISM ON PURGATORY

So what does the Roman Catholic Church say about purgatory? As I have already noted, the basic idea is that when Christians die they need to be cleaned up. They need to be purged of their sins.

They need to undergo a kind of punishment (which is claimed to be of a different sort than the kind the non-Christian will experience).[14] This punishment after death, they claim, will make Christians fit for seeing God and being in his presence.

For the Catholic leaders who teach about purgatory, the logic of this "necessary experience" begins with their understanding of sin. The *CCC* tells Catholics that there are two kinds of sins—*grave sins* (big sins) and *venial sins* (literally, "forgivable sins"). Every sin, even the small and forgivable sins, "must be purified either here on earth, or after death in the state called Purgatory."[15] They tell us that this purging is necessary "so as to achieve the holiness necessary to enter the joy of heaven."[16]

The words "either here on earth, or after death" may give Catholics a false hope that they could suffer enough for their sins in this life and get to bypass the fires of purgatory altogether. Though that loophole seems to exist in their official doctrinal statement, the word on the street from educated Catholics is "Don't get your hopes up!" Even though people talk about "hell on earth," most Catholics will tell you there is little chance you'll get to experience all of your "purgatory on earth."

Once, while in Rome, I stood in St. Peter's Square in Vatican City, in front of the Basilica, and decided to ask some of the seemingly important and high-ranking priests who were hurrying around whether they would help me understand purgatory. I asked, "Who goes to purgatory?" The answer I received was, "Everyone!" Standing in the shadow of the Pope's center of operations, who is said to represent Christ on earth, I sincerely inquired, "But what about the Pope? Are you telling me that His Holiness, as you call him, is going to be suffering in purgatory for some period of time when he dies?" A priest nodded and said, "Yes, of course." I followed with, "So you mean to tell me that there is not one good Catholic who gets to skip this terrible experience?" He paused, and said flippantly, "Well, maybe Mother Teresa."

That was another enlightening discussion for me with an educated and devoted priest. For one, because he seemed to believe that
Mother Teresa of Calcutta was more prepared for heaven than the
Vicar of Christ himself. And second, because if the Pope isn't going
to qualify for heaven without an extended trip to a fiery place called
purgatory, then certainly the average Catholic had better drop any
expectation that he or she is going to be exempt from this consign-
ment to suffer upon death.

But perhaps you are the kind of Bible believer who recognizes
the sole authority of Scripture.

SOLA SCRIPTURA

More than 500 years ago there was a growing frustration with the
leadership of the Church increasingly claiming the kind of authority that I have been describing. There were more and more out-
landish declarations being made about purgatory, penance,[17] and
indulgences.[18] Not only were the Church leaders progressively adding to the Scriptures, but those who had access to the Bible could
clearly see that these teachings were a contradiction to what Scripture plainly states.

From the early rumblings of John Wycliffe, John Huss, and the
Waldensians to the explosive impact of Martin Luther, John Calvin,
and Ulrich Zwingli, a growing band of Christians began to stand
up to the unbridled claims of the Church and began calling everyone back to the doctrinal boundaries of Scripture. The clergy of the
sixteenth century were being challenged by the simple quotations
and plain reading of the Bible. This is why people like William Tyndale had such a driving passion to get the Bible into the language
of the people. As historians say of this sixteenth-century Reformer:

> Many of the local clergy came to dine at the Walshes'
> manor, which gave Tyndale ample opportunity both

to be shocked by their ignorance of the Bible and to become embroiled in controversy with them. To one such cleric he declared: "If God spare my life, ere many years pass, I will cause a boy that driveth the plow shall know more of the Scripture than thou dost."[19]

The far-reaching impact of the Reformation, some 500 years ago, came down to a disagreement about authority. These brave men and women often paid for their courage with their lives. They were martyred for calling their peers and leaders to return to the authority of Scripture—the sole authority of Scripture! They said, and I hope we would echo, that if we are to know the truth about heaven, hell, and the afterlife, it will be found in the God-breathed pages of the Bible.

> *Purgatory is nowhere in the forecast for God's children.*

God has spoken about these supremely important matters, and any truth claim has to be weighed by the clear teaching of God's written Word. The church and her leaders cannot add to, subtract from, or in any way contradict what the Lord has settled in Scripture. This is why the "cry of the Reformation" was known in Latin as *Sola Scriptura*—"Scripture alone." And when it comes to purgatory, the authoritative words of the Bible give us a clear picture of what we are to expect. Purgatory is nowhere in the forecast for God's children.

QUALIFIED FOR HEAVEN

The New Testament has a lot to say about the things Christians are to be doing. We are, in the words of Colossians 1, to "walk in a manner worthy of the Lord" (verse 10), "bearing fruit in every good work," "increasing in the knowledge of God" (verse 10), and exemplifying "endurance and patience with joy" (verse 11). These are the types of things we work on as we progressively grow in the Christian life. God graciously works within us to produce these types of disciplines and virtues as we follow Christ. Hopefully we can all see this kind of forward momentum as we become more like Jesus in our thinking, words, and behavior. While we will never be sinless, until we arrive in heaven, the progressive call of the Christian life is to grow spiritually mature and sin less as the years roll by.

The New Testament also has a lot to say about the things Christians *already possess*. God has, in the words of Colossians 1, "qualified [us] to share in the inheritance of the saints in light" (verse 12), "delivered us from the domain of darkness" (verse 13), and "we have redemption, the forgiveness of sins" (verse 14). These are the things that *have been* accomplished and are granted to us, as verse 14 states "in whom"—that is, in the Father's "beloved Son" (verse 13). We have these things because of what Jesus has done for us. These are the things that have been achieved by Christ's life, death, and resurrection. These gifted realities are not progressive, they are finished, settled, and granted to us by faith.

This distinction in the Bible is crystal clear. The two categories are often distinguished by students of the Bible with the words *sanctification* and *justification*. By *sanctification* we refer to the progressive process of growing in Christ. This is associated in Scripture with the topic of rewards (as we will see in chapter 5). This process is something that takes place over time as God works within us, and as we respond to the varied commands and directives found in the Bible. By *justification* we refer to God's act of declaring us righteous at the very beginning of our Christian life. It speaks of that moment of being accepted as his adopted and forgiven child. This one-time act of justification is not based on any attempts on our part to be righteous. As the Bible tells us, this is based on the imputed or credited righteousness of Christ (Romans 4:1-8), and it is granted to us by faith (Philippians 3:4-9) and is not based on our good deeds (Ephesians 2:8-9).

Now back to Colossians 1. Here we have one of many passages that show the unmistakable difference between the things we seek to do as Christians and the foundational realities accomplished by Christ that made us Christians in the first place. Note the clear shift in the middle of this paragraph:

> From the day we heard, we have not ceased to pray for you, asking that you may be filled with the knowledge of his will in all spiritual wisdom and understanding, so as to walk in a manner worthy of the Lord, fully pleasing to him: bearing fruit in every good work and increasing in the knowledge of God; being strengthened with all power, according to his glorious might, for all endurance and patience with joy; giving thanks to the Father, who has qualified you to share in the inheritance of the saints in light. He has delivered us from the domain of darkness and transferred us to the kingdom of his beloved Son, in whom we have redemption, the forgiveness of sins (Colossians 1:9-14).

Yes, there are many things we seek to do as Christians, as the first half of this passage says—and as we make progress in those things, God will graciously reward us. But there are some things for which we can only give thanks because they are already done, they have already been granted, they have already been gifted to each Christian! Notice it again: We can only give thanks for our qualification, deliverance, and redemption that was achieved through Christ.

Just as we considered in the previous chapter, the thief on the cross had little time left to make progress in the Christian life. But, as God's Word makes clear, he was fully qualified for heaven; his status was transferred from darkness to light, and his redemption was gifted so that he could know he had the forgiveness of his sins. This man who had apparently spent his years engaged in serious crimes, was, at the moment of his faith in Christ, fully qualified for heaven! He, like us, had his sins forgiven and his legal status before God the Father was no longer considered to be in the domain of darkness. Instead, he was a full-fledged member of the kingdom of Christ.

Far better than a membership to some exclusive country club, the admission to God's kingdom has been fully paid. And if you have put your trust in Jesus Christ, you are completely qualified to enter. You at this very moment are no longer a nonmember; you are a fully qualified member! Your Father owns it, his Son has purchased your entry, and you have been robed in the qualifying garments of Christ's own righteousness!

THE DEBT IS FULLY PAID

When all of Christ's suffering was completed on the cross, and just before the moment of his death, Jesus said, "It is finished" (John 19:30). The payment for sins was "paid in full," as the single Greek term which translates this phrase was used in the financial world of his day. All the punishment that was due our sins was settled by that transaction on the cross. All the requirements of God's holiness and justice were completely resolved by the pain and suffering on that dark afternoon. It had the eternal impact of "canceling the record of debt that stood against us with its legal demands" (Colossians 2:14). There are no more legal demands to be made. There is no longer any punishment to be exacted. God took the record of debt away by "nailing it to the cross" (Colossians 2:14).

When the Romans crucified criminals, they listed their crimes and nailed them to the criminal's cross. The sight, I'm sure, was dramatic. "This is what these crimes led to!" Yet Jesus was without sin—at least without any of his own. The image of Colossians 2 transposes our crimes above the head of the Innocent One. Christ paid the penalty for our transgressions. Our moral crimes settled by his tortuous suffering. Yes, the Roman Catholics can be commended for understanding the gravity of sin. But how misguided and unbiblical not to recognize that the torture that justice demands has already been paid for by Jesus himself.

It would be as though you had been imprisoned in a high-security debtors' prison. Your financial crimes were piled high. The judge, the warden, and the prison guards all know you deserve to be locked up in that dark and dreadful place for the rest of your life. But some man, out of the great love with which he loved you, paid your debt in full. At great personal cost to himself, he came and delivered you from that dreary domain of darkness. At that point, you would no longer be rightly claimed by the debtors' prison. You have been set free. That warden and those guards have no more claim on your life. When Christ returns, the prison of this fallen earth, and its call to make you pay, will have no power to retain you. You've already been legally transferred. The accuser can only stand by as you are swept into the inheritance of the saints in light because you have already been fully qualified, and all your debts have been paid.

> God made us alive together with him, having forgiven us all our trespasses, by canceling the record of debt that stood against us with its legal demands. This he set aside, nailing it to the cross. He disarmed the rulers and authorities and put them to open shame, by triumphing over them in him (Colossians 2:13-15).

The spiritual entities who look on to shake their fist and demand that we pay for our sins are said to be shamed and defeated. The law of "crimes and punishments," of "cause and effect," of "sin and death," are all voided and defeated because his forgiven children are cleared by their Redeemer. There is no lingering punishment, no longer a reference to sins. Payment will not be required on account of the gracious salvation that was promised those who have trusted in him.

> …so Christ, having been offered once to bear the sins of many, will appear a second time, not to deal with sin but to save those who are eagerly waiting for him (Hebrews 9:28).

For Christians, the purification of our spirit before God has already taken place. Our sins have been removed from us as far as the east is from the west (Psalm 103:12). We no longer have our sins counted against us (Romans 4:5-8). That all happened instantaneously, just as it will happen to our fallen bodies. Our bodies will one day be transformed (Philippians 3:21). This change will not require some drawn-out process of purification. The Bible tells us that our sinful flesh will immediately put on immortality in a "twinkling of an eye" (1 Corinthians 15:51-52). For the Christian there is no expectation of a coming payment for sin.

> There is therefore now no condemnation for those who are in Christ Jesus. For the law of the Spirit of life has set you free in Christ Jesus from the law of sin and death (Romans 8:1-2).

Because our sins have been paid in full, there is no anticipation of punishment when we pass from this life. Instead, we "have confidence for the day of judgment" and not fear, "for fear has to do with punishment" (1 John 4:17-18). Yes, there will be a day of accountability for Christians—and there is much to say about that (see chapter 5)—but there is no fear of having to face the penalty of our transgressions. Yes, there will be an evaluation of each Christian life in order to expose all praiseworthy acts illustrated by the furnace's disclosing of "gold, silver, and precious stones," but there are no flames of torment in the afterlife for those whose sins have been appended to the cross of Christ.

While in this life we will all continue to experience the painful effects and consequences of sin, for the Christian the trials of living in our fallen world will come to an immediate end upon death. Because Christ has endured the agony of all that our sins deserve, there is no need for purgatory. Instead, we can look to the next life with joy and great anticipation.

> Though Satan should buffet, though trials should come;
> Let this blest assurance control,
> That Christ has regarded my helpless estate;
> And hath shed His own blood for my soul.
> My sin, oh, the bliss of this glorious thought!
> My sin, not in part but the whole,
> Is nailed to the cross, and I bear it no more;
> Praise the Lord, praise the Lord, O my soul![20]

CHAPTER 4

Heaven Is Filled with See-Through Bodies and Cotton-Ball Clouds

merican novelist and humorist Mark Twain was known to love the islands of Bermuda.[1] He was also known to say a lot of disparaging things about the Christian hope of the afterlife.[2] On one occasion Twain is famously quoted as comparing the two by saying, "You go to heaven if you want to, I'd rather stay right here in Bermuda."[3]

From his point of view, this ignorant statement makes perfect sense. Bermuda is full of beautiful sandy beaches and lush green golf courses. The weather is gorgeous, you can snorkel among colorful coral reefs, water-ski on pristine waters, walk along palm tree-lined harbors, and barbecue against the backdrop of stunning sunsets. And heaven, well...heaven, it's...well, it's a place...a place where the spirits of religious people go when they die, I guess.

If that's all we think of heaven, then of course we should all opt for Bermuda.

But if we do, we should remember that even Bermuda—great weather and all—is far from perfect. Right now as I write this I am looking at two websites listing the local news from there. I have clicked my way to the crime section. I am currently scrolling through long lists of headlines about stabbings, shootings, fistfights, robberies, gang activity, and more.

Leaving the crime section, I just clicked the "obituary" tabs on both websites. Guess what? People get sick there and die. Lots of them! I can be confident that everyone on that pristine island is facing the same ultimate prospect—sickness, suffering, and death.

Mark Twain himself was suffering from one final illness in Bermuda before he was hurriedly taken back to his home in Redding, Connecticut—where shortly thereafter he died. If only Twain were well informed about the reality of a perfect place, specifically crafted by the Master Builder to meet every need, without a hint of pain or suffering, death or sin. If only Twain would have maturely looked past the small-minded distortions concerning the true realities of our eternal home; I am quite sure he would have shared the ambition of the faith-filled men and women in Hebrews 11, who found this world's delights to be very small things in comparison to the perfection of what the Lord has laid up for his people.

> …having acknowledged that they were strangers and exiles on the earth. For people who speak thus make it clear that they are seeking a homeland. If they had been thinking of that land from which they had gone out, they would have had opportunity to return. But as it is, they desire a better country, that is, a heavenly one. Therefore God is not ashamed to be called their God, for he has prepared for them a city (Hebrews 11:13-16).

Like Abraham, we would all do well to be "looking forward to the city that has foundations, whose designer and builder is God" (Hebrews 11:10). But first we need to shed our ignorance about this place and know that our eternal home is not some ethereal or abstract experience with see-through bodies on cotton-ball clouds. Let's take a closer look at what God has said of this coming reality.

A NEW EARTH

Because Christians usually speak of their eternal home as heaven instead of as the new earth, it is easy to understand why so many immediately fall back to the imaginative images of cotton-ball clouds and see-through bodies. In the Bible we read of God's spiritual nature (as we considered in chapter 2); we are told that he is invisible by nature (Colossians 1:15; 1 Timothy 1:17); and that he "dwells in unapproachable light, whom no one has ever seen or can see" (1 Timothy 6:16). Then when we try to imagine being a part of that reality, it is next to impossible to do.

But God has revealed that we will one day have a resurrected body. The reconstituted physical bodies that we will inhabit, the Bible tells us, will be designed for a physical earth—a very tangible, solid, perceptible planet! Just beginning to think in terms of a new earth can begin to change everything about how we think of our eternal home. Revelation 21:1 tells us there will be a new heaven and a *new earth*. Dr. Robert Thomas comments,

> ...the appearance of the new heaven and earth is the disappearance of the first heaven and earth. The entrance of sin and death spoiled the earlier creation and made it a place of rebellion and alienation, an enemy-occupied territory. Its replacement with a whole new order of life without death, mourning, crying, and pain is a necessity.[4]

Pondering a nonfuzzy, nontransparent replacement earth filled with perfection can certainly make our obedience to Peter's exhortation much easier. He said we ought to be waiting for and hastening the coming of the day of God, because of which the heavens will be set on fire and dissolved.

The earth as we know it will be dissolved. But the earth as a tangible planet will be replaced with a "new earth in which righteousness dwells." I assume, with a little work, you can start to imagine and then truly begin to look forward to a fully righteous replacement version of the earth we all now occupy.

This new home should be so desirable for human beings, that God describes its introduction to his people like "a bride adorned for her husband" (Revelation 21:2). The replacement capital city is depicted in this verse as "coming down out of heaven from God, prepared as a bride adorned for her husband." Did you catch that? It is easy to miss the power of that verse because in the Bible, the bridal analogy refers to the church as the bride and to Christ as the husband. But in this passage the analogy of a bride's processional would have us envision ourselves as the husband, and the soon-to-arrive holy city as the beautiful bride.

In our day, you might appropriately imagine a scene in which an anxious and eager tuxedo-clad young man fixes his eyes on his beautiful bride as she enters the church adorned in a stunning wedding gown. In just about any culture, this marriage ceremony analogy mentioned in Revelation 21 works effectively well. There is hardly a scene more emotionally stirring than for us to begin to see that God is the architect and craftsman of a new planet that is perfectly suited and beautifully arrayed for his beloved and redeemed men and women.

A HOLY CITY

As I write this paragraph, I have just returned from speaking overseas at a church in downtown London. My experience of getting around town on the underground transit system in this burgeoning metropolis of thirteen million people wasn't easy. The train cars were frequently crowded, and one time I couldn't get on the first train that went by, and when I got on the next one, I was crammed like a sardine. It reminded me of the pictures I have seen of the sea of people on the train platform in Tokyo, or the thousands of people hanging onto the exterior of the trains in Mumbai. I live in a county of three million, and I know what it is like to regularly fight traffic on crowded freeways, but this London experience was overwhelming. At several points on this big-city trip I couldn't wait to get back to my tiny hotel room just to have a little breathing room and a few moments of peace and quiet.

A lot of us might get excited about what God is preparing for us in the next life when the Bible speaks of the new earth, but when we read there will also be a big city, there are some, I can only imagine, whose anticipation becomes deflated. Yet that is how God describes our new home. He tells us that the most beautiful thing about our future residence is not the countryside, but the jewel of the earth—the city called the New Jerusalem. Take in the Bible's description of it:

> He carried me away in the Spirit to a great, high mountain, and showed me the holy city Jerusalem coming down out of heaven from God, having the glory of God, its radiance like a most rare jewel, like a jasper, clear as crystal. It had a great, high wall, with twelve gates, and at the gates twelve angels, and on the gates the names of the twelve tribes of the sons of Israel were inscribed—on the east three gates, on the north three gates, on the south three gates, and on the west three gates. And the wall of the city had twelve foundations, and on them were the twelve names of the twelve apostles of the Lamb. And the one who spoke with me had a measuring rod of gold to measure the city and its gates and walls. The city lies foursquare, its length the same as its width. And he measured the city with his rod, 12,000 stadia. Its length and width and height are equal (Revelation 21:10-16).

This is no ordinary big city. For one, it is spread out—"12,000 stadia" is the ancient measurement equivalent to roughly 1,400 miles. Wherever you are, think of a place on the map that is approximately 1,400 miles from where you are right now. That is the squared area (actually the cubed area) of this jewel of the new earth. I imagine that the density of this urban center will be nothing like what I recently experienced in that crowded subway station.

One reason we often have an aversion to big cities is because of the rude, pushy, filthy, selfish, and criminal elements within those cities. You have to watch your back, protect your wallet, fight for your place in line. Yet millions of people choose to live in the big cities of our fallen earth because they find it worth all the precautions just to have close access to all the shops, restaurants, businesses, museums, and civic interests.

We are told that this city will shine with "the glory of God" (verse 11). It is described a few verses earlier as having "the dwelling place of God" in it (verse 3). I take this specifically to be Christ, who will forever exist in his tangible and truly physical resurrected body. He is the One described as "the radiance of the glory of God and the exact imprint of his nature" (Hebrews 1:3). Of course, God the Father and God the Holy Spirit will be, and are, everywhere present. And God will be unmitigated and unencumbered in his glory in that place, but the visible King of the city will be Jesus himself, enthroned in the center of this perfect metropolis. This will be the ideal kind of city living, with access to Christ himself!

Not only will God's glory be on display in Christ, in the way it was ever so briefly during the transfiguration (Matthew 17:1-3), but there will be no rude, pushy, filthy, selfish, or criminal elements in this new city (Revelation 21:8). God has promised to "wipe away every tear" from our eyes—there will be no mourning, crying, or pain in our new home (verse 4).

PHYSICAL BODIES

We should have no doubt that the bodies we will possess in that big city will be physical. And they will not be semitransparent or see-through. We know this because the Bible tells us that Christ's resurrected body is the prototype, or "firstfruits," of the ones that

God will reconstitute for us (1 Corinthians 15:20, 23). So to learn about our future bodies, we can go to the accounts of how Jesus's risen body functioned.

After his resurrection, Jesus insisted that the startled disciples should touch his body to prove that they were not hallucinating or having some sort of vision. They were certainly shocked to see Jesus standing before them, knowing that just a few days earlier they had watched him be tortured and killed. Luke records their encounter:

> They were startled and frightened and thought they saw a spirit. And he said to them, "Why are you troubled, and why do doubts arise in your hearts? See my hands and my feet, that it is I myself. Touch me, and see. For a spirit does not have flesh and bones as you see that I have" (Luke 24:37-39).

"Flesh and bones." That's how Jesus described his resurrected body. This was no see-through translucent apparition. He had an elbow, a kneecap, a hip bone, and a spinal cord. He had fingernails, hair, ears, and toes. He existed in a real, physical, flesh-and-bone body. What he did next should have put any doubts to rest. Luke tells us that Jesus "said to them, 'Have you anything here to eat?' They gave him a piece of broiled fish, and he took it and ate before them" (verses 41-43).

Think of it—real teeth, a tongue with taste buds, a working esophagus, and a stomach capable of digesting a chewed-up piece of broiled fish. He had a fully functioning physical body, and so will you! His body is the prototype of your future resurrected body, as physical as they come. Different in many ways from your current body, but certainly and truly physical.

PERFECTED BODIES

The Bible contrasts the experience we all now know in our failing bodies with the future reality we will know in our resurrected bodies. The following passage of Scripture reveals to us four radical distinctions between the bodies we have now and the ones that we will have as we enter the New Jerusalem.

> Someone will ask, "How are the dead raised? With what kind of body do they come?" You foolish person!...What is sown is perishable; what is raised is imperishable. It is sown in dishonor; it is raised in glory. It is sown in weakness; it is raised in power. It is sown a natural body; it is raised a spiritual body (1 Corinthians 15:35-36, 42-44).

1. They Will Be Ageless

The word "perishable" in verse 42 always reminds me of the problem I have with bananas. I like to eat a banana almost every day. The problem is, I am one of those people who likes them only when they are "just right." I don't like them green, obviously. But I also don't like them if they are even the slightest bit overripe. I don't like banana bread, and I can't stand my bananas mushy—not in the least bit. It seems to me like bananas are "just right" for only about three or four hours. Why? Because they are perishable—really perishable! And it seems that they start perishing the minute after they fully ripen.

> God's promise is that the perfectly remanufactured bodies he will craft for us will be imperishable.

I hate to compare our bodies to a perishing banana. But depending on how old we are as we read this sentence, I think most of us can agree the prime of life passes quickly and our fallen bodies get "mushy" before we know it. Our skin, our hair, our bones, our joints—they all start falling apart just as quickly as they grew to full maturity. God's promise is that the perfectly remanufactured bodies he will craft for us will be imperishable. How fantastic to imagine possessing a perfected anatomy that is impervious to disease, decay, aging, and any sort of deterioration or physical decline.

People often ask, "What age will we be?" By that I assume people mean to ask, "What age will our bodies appear to be?" I can only speculate that our bodies will be fully mature and wholly developed—logically, this seems like what our bodies were designed to achieve and what we, in futility, fight to maintain. Everything in our youthful physical development aims toward that maturity, and all that comes after this point feels and appears to be a detrimental and painful detraction from it. But as to age, there will be none—our bodies will be ageless in the sense that they will no longer be perishable. We will live in the ideal physical development of what bodies are to be—not "green" and not "mushy"!

Of course, in this life, even the best physical specimen among us reaches his or her peak with a number of imperfections. Most of us experience problems even when we are in our prime. But when it comes to our resurrected body, we can say good-bye to allergies, migraines, asthma, near- or farsightedness, diabetes, or any other defect. Our resurrected bodies will not be subject to such things. God will reconstitute them without a single physical imperfection. Praise God, our aches and pains, aging and diseases will be no more.

2. They Will Be Beautiful

It would make sense that imperishable bodies will be beautiful. The word used in 1 Corinthians 15:43 to describe our future bodies is "glory." That word has a wide variety of applications in the Bible, all the way from the significant importance of a matter to the absolute perfection of God himself. In this context, however, it speaks a striking appearance.

This was the same word Jesus used when he spoke to crowds who were concerned about how they looked due to the quality and beauty of their clothing. He pointed them to the lilies of the field and said, "I tell you, even Solomon in all his glory was not arrayed like one of these" (Matthew 6:29). We can be sure that the richest king in the Bible possessed the finest royal robes money could buy. Certainly he took pains to look regal, important, and handsome, presenting himself in a manner that befits monarchs. But Jesus said that the flowers of the field are even more glorious, even better looking.

When the Bible says that our resurrected bodies will be "raised in glory," we get a sense that we can anticipate a physical appearance that is stunning, resplendent, and glorious. Whatever now makes our bodies physically dishonorable will be radically reconstructed to be objectively beautiful.

I should point out that this does not mean we will look identical. Pretty eyes, handsome shoulders, or a beautiful smile certainly don't need to be indistinguishable from everyone else's to be glorious. I think we can all readily admit that God's glory in creation is manifest (even in this imperfect world) with a great deal of variety. Varied heights, an assortment of hair color, a variety of skin tones, and various face shapes and contours can all easily be envisioned as faultlessly beautiful and perfectly attractive, yet exceedingly diverse.

3. They Will Be Tireless

Next, we are told in 1 Corinthians 15 that though our current bodies are characterized by weakness, our reconstructed bodies will be raised in power. The Bible often reminds us that our bodies are weak, prone to fatigue, and often uncooperative when we go about our lives. Even now, as I write this sentence, I am tired. Perhaps you are tired as you read it. I am experiencing jet lag from my recent overseas speaking engagement, wearied from answering emails, sore from moving furniture this morning, and I am feeling the physical necessity of taking a 15-minute break from writing this chapter. Even when we have strong intentions of doing something good, our bodies are so often obstinate in their weakness.

Jesus said as much to the disciples in the garden, who were told to stay awake and pray with Christ in his most distressing hour. Yet, as the Bible states, "their eyes were heavy" and they failed to watch and pray (Matthew 26:43). Their intentions were good, and I am sure they purposed to meet the need. But like us, even when the spirit is willing, the flesh is weak (Mark 14:38).

Thankfully, one day all that will be a thing of the past. God has promised that our resurrected bodies will be characterized by "power." The Greek word translated "power" in 1 Corinthians 15:43 is also used in 2 Corinthians 1:8—there, Paul spoke of his afflictions in Asia, which led to him be so burdened beyond his strength that he despaired of life itself. He felt as though he had no power or strength to continue. Our resurrected bodies will always have a surplus of physical power. They will be fueled and empowered to do what our regenerate spirits purpose to do. Our bodies will no longer be weak impediments; they will then be our strong and capable allies.

4. They Will Want to Do Right

When it comes to doing right, we are not used to our body being an ally. It often acts as an enemy. It is a "fallen body," we often say, because it has a propensity for doing the wrong thing. Not only does our body lack strength, but so often it is energized by what is sinful. Temptation so often ignites our flesh and it is drawn to do what we know is unrighteous. For the Christian, this is a constant frustration. Peter said the passions of our flesh wage war against our souls (1 Peter 2:11). This is the problem that the fourth contrast in 1 Corinthians 15 addresses.

We are told that our resurrected bodies will no longer be "natural." Rather, they will be "spiritual" (1 Corinthians 15:44). Here is where many Christians have picked up a wrong idea. When people hear that our future bodies will be "spiritual," they often think of see-through bodies, invisible spirits, or phantoms. But as we have already seen, our resurrected bodies will be physical and tangible, just like Christ's resurrected body. So it is important to understand the word "spiritual" the same way we do in Galatians 6, where Paul wrote that "if anyone is caught in any transgression, you who are spiritual should restore him in a spirit of gentleness" (verse 1).

I don't think anyone reads that verse and looks for the Christian with the most translucent body. No, when we read the word "spiritual," we think *godly*, *devout*, and *mature*. In almost every context, when someone says a person is spiritual, he or she is talking about someone who lives in a godly way and is progressing in sanctification. So when the Bible says that our future bodies will be "spiritual," we should breathe a sigh of relief. It means there is coming a day when we will no longer battle our fleshly inclinations to do wrong. The natural tendencies we struggle with now are spelled out in passages like this one:

> Now the works of the flesh are evident: sexual immorality, impurity, sensuality, idolatry, sorcery, enmity, strife, jealousy, fits of anger, rivalries, dissensions, divisions, envy, drunkenness, orgies, and things like these (Galatians 5:19-21).

Imagine every fight with temptation that is currently fueled by your fallen flesh. It will be gone! Every unrighteous lust, every sinful desire, every passion that draws you to do what is sinful—absent from your resurrected body! That is good news, and something you and I should eagerly anticipate.

PERFECT SATISFACTION

Speaking of desires, there are plenty of good and righteous desires that you now experience. When you became a Christian, the Bible says you were given a new heart and a new spirit (Ezekiel 36:26; Colossians 3:9-10). With that new interior you were given a new set of desires. Everything was reoriented within you (2 Corinthians 5:17). Those "core desires," as I like to call them, will all be perfectly satisfied. As the psalmist said to the Lord: "You make known to me the path of life; in your presence there is fullness of joy; at your right hand are pleasures forevermore" (Psalm 16:11). The good and righteous longings and cravings will be completely fulfilled when you are situated in the city where Christ lives.

This picture is painted for us with the imagery of God feeding and nourishing us with his presence and his abundant provisions.

> The angel showed me the river of the water of life, bright as crystal, flowing from the throne of God and of the Lamb through the middle of the street of the city; also, on either side of the river, the tree of life with its twelve kinds of fruit, yielding its fruit each month. The leaves of the tree were for the healing of the nations. No longer will there be anything accursed, but the throne of God and of the Lamb will be in it, and his servants will worship him (Revelation 22:1-3).

There will be no disappointment, no deprivation, and no depression. We will be fed in every sense, and will react with sincere praise and worship. We won't have to command our spirit to worship God as we so often do now (Psalm 103:1-2). We will joyfully react with thanksgiving with full hearts and well-fed lives.

NO BOREDOM

Mentioning *worship* in the afterlife can surface a silent concern—namely, that we will be stuck in an endless worship service in the New Jerusalem, forced to sing the lyrics of every worship song ever written. And we're afraid that even when we are done, we will be directed to start singing them all over again. Even those with the best of experiences in earthly worship services will tell you that there is an appropriate time to wrap up the meeting and move out to grab some lunch or read a book.

If your unspoken aversion to thinking about the afterlife is prompted by this concern, allow me to relieve your fears. Even in this life, the exaltation of God is not confined to the singing of worship songs. The Bible says that you can and should seek to glorify God even when you are having dinner (1 Corinthians 10:31). In your daily tasks and at your place of employment, the Bible says you are to be engaged in consciously and joyfully serving Christ no matter what your job title might be.

> Whatever you do, work heartily, as for the Lord and not for men, knowing that from the Lord you will receive the inheritance as your reward. You are serving the Lord Christ (Colossians 3:23-24).

Our ongoing existence in our eternal home is described in a similar way in Revelation 7:15 and 22:3. There are two primary words in the Greek New Testament which translate to our English word *worship*. One is often utilized in contexts where men and women are bowing down, singing, or expressing their praise directly to God. The other Greek word is used in these two verses in Revelation and describes our future experience, speaks of people engaging in tasks and activities to the praise and glory of God.[5] Yes, we can expect to sing and express our praise directly to God (in that place, without any resistance from our hearts or flesh), but we can also expect to be engaged in activities that will honor God.

Some of those activities are described in the Bible as assignments of leadership. Revelation 22:5 says we "will reign forever," and Revelation 2:26-27 speak of being given "authority." Leading people or projects is certainly not boring. And if you say, "I was hoping to be assigned a beach chair and a hammock between two palm trees," I would remind you that the reason we recoil from leadership responsibilities in this fallen world is because fallen people and sinful circumstances tend to make such responsibilities frustrating and difficult to carry out.

Remember that after sin entered the world, God told Adam that work would involve "pain" and "sweat" (Genesis 3:17-19). But don't forget that before Adam and Eve's fall into sin, the world in which Adam was called to work was without either of those negative realities. In other words, the work assigned to Adam prior to the fall could be described as "no sweat" and "pain free"! In our new home, that will be true again.

If every task in heaven wherein you could engage your creativity, apply your wisdom, and purpose your mind to work had no pain, frustration, or disappointment associated with it, I'm assuming you would rethink your ambition of lounging in a hammock for eternity. Thoughtful students of the Bible have explored this topic in books that allow much more space to develop what this might include. Those might be worth exploring as you anticipate your eternal home.[6] If you do, you'll find that everyone who defers to Scripture, and not to the ignorant myths of our culture, comes to the same conclusion: God's plans for our lives on the new earth are compelling, spectacular, and interesting. We have much to look forward to.

A PLACE FOR GOD'S PEOPLE

It would be negligent of me to go on about how great and very real this New Jerusalem will be without taking a minute to make sure you are going there. I know it may seem more appropriate to discuss this when I describe the realities of hell later in this book, but how awful it would be for you to resonate with the pleasures and fulfillments of the new earth and not actually be qualified for it.

Some of the most tragic words in the New Testament have to be those from Jesus when he disclosed that many who expect to enter his kingdom will be surprised that they are not welcome (Matthew 7:21-23). Instead of hearing, "Come, you who are blessed by my Father, inherit the kingdom prepared for you from the foundation of the world" (Matthew 25:34), they will hear, "Depart from me, you cursed, into the eternal fire prepared for the devil and his angels" (verse 41).

Elsewhere, Jesus referred to a man attempting to attend a wedding feast (you can hardly imagine a more festive occasion with which to compare the coming kingdom), but because he was not dressed in the appropriate attire, he could not attend (Matthew 22:11-13). I want to make sure you are ready. Are you clothed in Christ's righteousness (Galatians 3:27)? Have you trusted wholly in the finished work of Jesus on the cross? Are you holding on to your sins and idols, which are you unwilling to relinquish? Have you seen your sin for what it is and do you recognize that your only hope for life on God's new earth is faith in Christ?

I appeal for you to receive Christ as your Savior so that you may enter the place God has promised to construct for his people. Give up the foolishness of this world and all its expectations, and be counted with Jesus. Repent of your sins and place your trust in Jesus Christ to save you! He will personally guarantee you a place in this amazing future home.

CHAPTER 5

Heaven Is Filled with Tract Homes and Government-Issued Uniforms

imagine heaven is filled with tract homes and government-issued uniforms." Okay, you may not say it that way, but I have interacted with enough Christians over the years to know that many think of our eternal home as a place where everyone has an equal amount of everything, equal access to every place, equal ownership of whatever it is that is there, and everyone enjoys an equal set of privileges. But before you settle into that all-too-common perspective, let's give it some thought and compare it to what the Bible actually says about our future home.

NO CELESTIAL COMMUNISM

There is no doubt that the most important thing we could possibly consider is whether or not we will have any place in the future eternal kingdom of God. I can understand the sentiment that says, "I will just be glad I'm in!" But God has repeatedly told us to give thought, effort, and regular concern as to what sort of place we will have in his coming kingdom.

To envision the New Jerusalem as a city with rows of cookie-cutter homes, identical yards, matching forms of transportation in the driveway, filled with people on their porches wearing matching outfits with the same haircut, is to completely overlook much of the teaching of the Bible about our future—and the present! As theologian Wayne Grudem repeatedly points out, the modern theories of communism and socialism are contradictory to biblical teaching about human dignity and the God-given gifts of freedom and choice.[1] If these principles apply now, their relevance would certainly not end with this life. In fact, the Bible explicitly tells us they do not.

When Jesus speaks on issues related to the afterlife, he regularly calls us to consider our placement in his kingdom and to do what we can to positively invest in it. First and foremost, he wants us to make sure we are going there. Then he desires that we apply ourselves now so that we will flourish there:

> Do not lay up for yourselves treasures on earth, where moth and rust destroy and where thieves break in and steal, but lay up for yourselves treasures in heaven, where neither moth nor rust destroys and where thieves do not break in and steal. For where your treasure is, there your heart will be also (Matthew 6:19-21).

The problem identified in these words from Christ is not the storing up of treasure; it is, rather, that we are prone to working at storing it up in the wrong place. Because the Bible speaks so often to the foolishness of investing in the sinking ship of this world, people with a casual acquaintance of Scripture tend to think that to be like Jesus is to lack ambition, focus, and a desire for achievement. But to have that perspective is to miss Christ's call to get to work at investing in our future home.

A building project around the corner from our church is just finishing up. The builders have been constructing a beautiful six-story, state-of-the-art, 220,000-square-foot office complex on a five-acre lot. For months I have watched the progress each day as I drove past the site on my way to the church office. As with most large construction sites, the foreman had a trailer set up on the edge of the lot as his center of operations from day to day. Every week I would see the light on in that trailer, or activity up and down the steps leading into this nondescript office. As the months went by, the sparkling new office complex rose skyward. Just the other day I was driving by when a big rig was hooking up the now-empty trailer-office to haul it away.

I couldn't help but think this was no surprise to anyone. The six-story office complex was the focus and the goal. The trailer was just a temporary workspace. I never saw the construction workers add any decorations to the little deck next to its entrance. I can only assume the trailer was modestly equipped. Sure, it probably had a fan, a desk, a cabinet, maybe a little refrigerator—and who knows, perhaps the foreman's favorite seascape hung on the wall. But I can assure you the planning, attention, concern, and all the daily labor was focused on the job that lay just outside the flimsy walls of that small office. I'm confident the foreman never forgot why he was there. He wasn't relaxing in his temporary office trying to experience the good life. He wasn't loafing around all day. Nor was he investing all his time and effort in adorning his makeshift workspace to make it as luxurious as possible. No, I can safely suppose that he was a hard worker with the bigger and most important goal in view—putting up that other building!

Obviously, Jesus would have us do the same.

There is a permanent reality coming for which God wants you and I to prepare. Not only by making sure we are genuine Christians and having our living space reserved, but also by applying ourselves and prioritizing our lives so that the spot we settle into is one we've been investing in for years. The one difference I should add to the construction foreman story is that in our case, we will be moving into that office complex. Our work is not only for the glory of the Investor who underwrites the project, God has so arranged things that the investments we make now from this temporary trailer called earth will be storing up for us benefits and privileges that we ourselves will enjoy when we occupy that place.

SELFISH?

Whenever I preach on passages about storing up treasures in heaven (Matthew 6:20), or texts that say that God rewards those who earnestly seek him (Hebrews 11:6), or when I teach on Christ's statements that the one who sacrifices for his disciples "he will by no means lose his reward" (Matthew 10:42), or verses that say, in keeping the Lord's commands, "there is great reward" (Psalm 19:11), Christians often come up to me with the objection that it all sounds way too selfish and self-serving. How can we give attention and effort to the work of the Christian life with any thoughts of future compensation? Shouldn't we just serve to serve? Shouldn't we just sacrifice because it is the right thing to do? Shouldn't we graciously obey God without expecting anything in return?

If you were to hear the balance of my preaching you would hear plenty of sermons that expound passages which say just that. Of course we should live to the glory of God no matter what it costs, because he deserves it. We should even get to the place where we so understand the grace of salvation and the grace of his kindness to reward us that we can sincerely echo this oft-neglected passage: "So you also, when you have done all that you were commanded, say, 'We are unworthy servants; we have only done what was our duty'" (Luke 17:10). We have a duty to live for Christ, and it is a duty that we must discharge regardless. Like Shadrach, Meshach, and Abednego, we should resolve to do what God commands regardless of whether he delivers us or rewards us, either now or in the next life (Daniel 3:16-18).

All of that is true, and yet God has promised to reward us. Even from the very beginning of our lives, the command given for children to obey their parents is delivered with the motivation of a reward (Ephesians 6:1-3). Jesus often injected the righteous and proper motivation of repayment in the afterlife, to encourage selfless and godly behavior in this life:

> When you give a feast, invite the poor, the crippled, the lame, the blind, and you will be blessed, because they cannot repay you. For you will be repaid at the resurrection of the just (Luke 14:13-14).

Those who are in heaven watching the end-time events unfold will sing that it is "the time for the dead to be judged, and for rewarding your servants" (Revelation 11:18). And Jesus himself declared on the final page of the Bible: "I am coming soon, bringing my recompense with me, to repay each one for what he has done" (Revelation 22:12). This has been the theme throughout the Bible: "Surely there is a reward for the righteous; surely there is a God who judges on earth" (Psalm 58:11). In the Christian life we are compared to athletes who strive to store up awards, medals, and trophies. The difference between them and us, the Bible declares, is that "they do it to receive a perishable wreath, but we an imperishable" (1 Corinthians 9:25).

For all the objections I receive to the biblical teachings about eternal rewards, I am amazed at how many of these same Christians march back home only to immediately apply the same principle to their own children as it relates to this life. The same Christians who claim it is all too self-serving and selfish to be motivated in any way by the promise of future rewards boldly tell their children to work hard in school, diligently do their homework, study for exams, and apply themselves in all that they do so that they can land good jobs and make a better wage in their adult lives.

If we can be righteous and principled parents by teaching our kids the cause-and-effect of hard work and discipline in this life, it is hard to understand why we cry foul when Jesus says this about eternal life. We must stop rejecting the clear teaching of Scripture regarding how we live our Christian lives. If our children can be taught the future value of today's hard work, sacrifice, and diligence without damaging our virtue as Christians, then of course we should live by the same biblical concepts as it relates to eternity.

With regard to our children, when we truly understand the enduring value of eternal rewards, we may rethink the way we motivate them about schooling and career rewards. It may be that we are creating ambitious and disciplined kids who can see the horizon of their professional careers but not beyond. The doctrine of eternal rewards may in fact change a lot about our goals pertaining to this "temporary trailer" in which we now live.

TRUE RICHES AND REAL GREATNESS

As we have seen, ambition is not the problem. Rather, the Bible warns us to not misplace our ambition. While the world tells us and our children to expect great things from yourself and attempt great things for yourself, we are instead biblically encouraged to share the ambition expressed by the missionary William Carey, who said, "Expect great things *from God*; attempt great things *for God*!"[2]

We would find ourselves so much better aligned with Christ's instructions were we to desire the spiritual ambitions expressed by D.L. Moody when he wired these words to the parents of his fourth granddaughter: "May she become famous in the Kingdom of Heaven."[3] Reading the Bible carefully, not selectively, will surely leave us with the same impression as C.S. Lewis, who wrote: "If we consider the unblushing promises of reward and the staggering nature of the rewards promised in the Gospels, it would seem that Our Lord finds our desires not too strong, but too weak."[4]

In the Bible, self-promoting prideful ambition is condemned as sinful (James 3:14-15). And much of the initiative, drive, and serious determination we see in those around us is shortsighted and will result in nothing 1,000 years from now. But for all the secular abuses, the disciple of Jesus must hear the wisdom of Christ to exchange these ambitions for a higher one—a quest for what he called "true riches" and real greatness (Luke 16:11; Matthew 5:19). John Wesley was right when he hinted that our dismal response to Christ's teaching on rewards may be a cover for our own laziness. Note here his comments as he considers the varied rewards granted to the saints in the book of Revelation:

> Let not any slothful one say, "If I get to heaven at all, I will be content"…In worldly things men are ambitious to get as high as they can. Christians have a far more noble ambition.[5]

The materialistic ambitions that motivate people in this life often result in them hoarding earth's limited resources to the hurt of others. They store up treasure on earth, failing to be generous and refusing to understand that their specific advantages in life should prompt them to give and to share with those who are without those advantages. But heaven's resources are endless. The wealth and resources of the new earth are unlimited. You can't store up treasure in heaven to the hurt of others. And this life's "advantages" become all but irrelevant when it comes to eternal rewards because of the basis on which they are granted—our faithfulness, and not our innate intelligence, nor our pedigree, nor our location on the planet, nor the era in which we were born. In other words, the one who faithfully applies himself with the little he has been entrusted can store up the same kind of abundant treasure as the one who faithfully applies himself with the massive amount of influence or intelligence he has been given. All of us, regardless of our gifts and abilities, should excitedly heed the call to store up treasure in heaven.

Let us be done with saying that being motivated by God's promised rewards is sinful. Let us be quick to remember the loving and relational context in which these promises are given. Imagine that I told my junior high son I would throw a huge pizza and pool party for him and his friends if he was diligent to do his homework and got a certain number of *A*s on his report card. Let's say he worked hard and achieved those grades. I would be more than happy to throw the promised party. And I would also be pleased if the promise of my reward motivated him to get those grades.

> *All of us, regardless of our gifts and abilities, should excitedly heed the call to store up treasure in heaven.*

Now if he refused to work hard that semester *unless* I rewarded him with the pizza and pool party, that would be wrong—he should do what I have asked him to do anyway. On the other hand, it would be wrong of him, and disappointing for me—as well as altogether foolish—if he told me, "I'm going to work hard, but I don't want any of your rewards."

When our heavenly Father lovingly offers the motivation of eternal rewards, we would do well to keep those promises in view. Sure, any good motive can be distorted. An unbalanced pursuit of the fulfillment of the promises of God can degenerate into something crass. And so we must guard our hearts when Jesus calls us to "store up treasure in heaven." But we must not set this pursuit aside. God's promised rewards are not the only motive for serving him, loving his people, or seeking first his kingdom and his righteousness, but being motivated by them is biblical. Just as a good son will obey his parents to please them, it is also a righteous and good ambition for that son to look to the benefits which God has graciously and lovingly tied to his commands.

THE REWARDS

It is difficult to be specific about the exact nature of the rewards that are held out to us in the Bible because there is much we were not told about the everyday experience in the New Jerusalem. But let's look at what is hinted at by the words used in Scripture to motivate us in our daily Christian life. Before we look the specific types of rewards, let's focus on the ultimate gift, which is the centerpiece of every reward mentioned in the Bible.

1. God Himself

We get God. There is nothing greater than having an unmitigated and personal connection with the Source of all joy. Psalm 16:11 says of God, "In your presence there is fullness of joy; at your right hand are pleasures forevermore." For now, as the New Testament says, "We see in a mirror dimly, but then face to face" (1 Corinthians 13:12). The greatest experiences we've had in prayer, Bible study, or worship are nothing compared to what we will experience when we have the glorified Christ in the middle of the city in which we live (Revelation 21:3).

Once I say this, you may be back to questioning Wesley's logic. Maybe that *is* all that will matter. Perhaps, if you get to heaven at all, you will be content. And in a sense you will be, but that is not the whole picture. Imagine I called you and told you that I had arranged a dinner for you with the person you respect the most in our generation—a sports star, some renown scholar, a celebrity, or a favorite musician. I've prepared everything—all you have to do is show up at the arranged time and place. I assume you would be excited. You would consider it a privilege, and perhaps even see it as a "bucket list" meeting.

Now let's imagine that the arranged meal included a bucket—a bucket of chicken on a park bench. I hope you'd still be excited to be with the person you so greatly admire. You would take pictures, tell your friends the next day, post a few quotes from the meal on social media. No big deal that you were eating with your hands and wiping them on a paper napkin that you had to tuck under your leg so it wouldn't fly away in the wind.

Now let's rethink this scenario. Imagine that the meeting with this VIP wasn't on a drive-thru meal budget. You roll up to the pre-arranged spot and it happens to be the most luxurious restaurant in the state. The table is by the window, which offers an amazing view. The chairs are the most comfortable you've ever sat in. The menu is filled with your favorite dishes, and the service from the tuxedo-clad waiters is impeccable. Again, I imagine you would take pictures, remember quotes, and tell your friends what an incredible meeting it was. But in this imaginary situation the *incredible* is even more amazing.

I know every Christian's experience with Christ in eternity is going to be terrific. But there is a different category of *terrific* based on Christ's rewards. No one will be dissatisfied or lacking. But you would have to admit that there is a kind of meal that gratifies and satisfies, and there are meals that gratify and satisfy even more. I know there is some mystery to it all. What will it be like to live with God? It will be great—for everyone. But the varied quantity and quality of the rewards we are about to try to imagine will undoubtedly increase our gratification and satisfaction. No one will regret "storing up" these kinds of additions to the experience of living in the presence of Christ.

2. Reputation

One of the first distinctions frequently talked about in the Bible is that of our eternal reputation. Few things will matter more in

our new home than God's assessment of our lives. According to
1 Corinthians 3, the deeds and actions of our Christian lives will be
compared to a composite of gold, silver, precious stones, wood, hay,
and straw (verse 12). On the day our lives are analyzed (2 Corinthians 5:9-10), the worthless wood, hay, and straw investments will be
found to be inconsequential, while the gold, silver, and precious
stone investments will be richly rewarded (1 Corinthians 3:14). We
are told that this reward begins with a commendation or praise from
God (1 Corinthians 4:5).

Just as in this life you care what the people you love think of you,
so the acclaim God grants your Christian life on *that day* will be of
supreme importance—not just to you, but to others. The extent
to which God congratulates his servants will not be kept a secret
between the two of them. Consider the forecast we have already
received about God's view of the twelve apostles. We are given this
description of their fame:

> The wall of the city had twelve foundations, and on them
> were the twelve names of the twelve apostles of the Lamb
> (Revelation 21:14).

Here we have billboards prominently displaying the names
of a select set of individuals. Can you imagine passing by these
names on the new earth? There will be no getting around the fame
of these twelve. Yet even among them there will be a ranking of varied reputations. Jesus spoke to this when two of the twelve asked for
prominence in the next life. Notice how Jesus tied these places of
distinction to the sacrifices they would endure for him:

> James and John, the sons of Zebedee, came up to him
> and said to him, "Teacher, we want you to do for us
> whatever we ask of you." And he said to them, "What
> do you want me to do for you?" And they said to him,

"Grant us to sit, one at your right hand and one at your left, in your glory." Jesus said to them, "You do not know what you are asking. Are you able to drink the cup that I drink, or to be baptized with the baptism with which I am baptized?" And they said to him, "We are able." And Jesus said to them, "The cup that I drink you will drink, and with the baptism with which I am baptized, you will be baptized, but to sit at my right hand or at my left is not mine to grant, but it is for those for whom it has been prepared" (Mark 10:35-40).

If ever there was a time to correct any misguided thinking about prominence or standing in eternity, this was it. But instead of saying, "Hey guys, everyone is equal in the next life," Jesus told them that the way it is achieved is not by asking for it, but by living a life that is willing to sacrifice and even suffer for his cause.

You may be tempted to say, "I'll be happy to be a nobody in the New Jerusalem," but I would challenge that thinking and call you never to turn your nose up at Christ's call to be great in the kingdom (Matthew 20:26-27). The godly fame and righteous reputation God will grant to his hardworking and sacrificial servants will forever be celebrated in eternity (Daniel 12:3). Don't plan to sneak into the kingdom as a nobody. As Peter commands, "make every effort" to live the kind of life that provides a rich and hearty welcome into the eternal kingdom of our Lord (2 Peter 1:5-11).

3. Responsibilities

As I mentioned in the last chapter, your gut-reaction to the word *responsibility* in any kingdom might be "No thanks!" But please remember that the reason you don't want to sign up to be on the homeowners' association board or to volunteer for that leadership position in the community is because you currently live in a fallen, broken, messed-up world. It is filled with sin and sinners—which means that even the most virtuous responsibilities, in the best situations possible, will be overseen by the sweat of your brow with the pricks and pokes of thorns and thistles (Genesis 3:18-19). But it won't be so in the New Jerusalem.

In Matthew 19:22, a rich young ruler walked away from the call to follow Christ because the price tag was too high. Evidently Peter had taken note of Jesus's words to the young man about the potential of "treasure in heaven" (verse 21), for Peter said to Jesus, "See, we have left everything and followed you. What then will we have?" (verse 27).

Again, at this point, if Jesus were needing to correct wrong thinking about rewards, it was the perfect time. He could have said, "Stop thinking about what's in it for you!" Instead, Jesus laid out the heady promise of increased responsibilities that Peter and the others were "storing up" for themselves through their sacrificial service for him:

> Jesus said to them, "Truly, I say to you, in the new world, when the Son of Man will sit on his glorious throne, you who have followed me will also sit on twelve thrones, judging the twelve tribes of Israel" (Matthew 19:28).

Wow. A mix of former fishermen, wild-eyed zealots, and turncoat tax collectors were promised responsibilities of the oversight of the entire nation of Israel. Talk about a job promotion! These men had laid down their lives and livelihoods to become poor traveling associates of a hunted and outcast Messiah, and at the same time, their costly investment was earning unimaginable career dividends for the next life.

This was a common theme in Jesus's preaching. His parables often included the idea of hardworking followers one day hearing the words, "You have been faithful over a little; I will set you over much. Enter into the joy of your master" (Matthew 25:21).

What decisions will you make this week that will change your job title in eternity? What spiritual priorities will lead you to start making careful choices that will affect the wording on your business card in the kingdom? What investment might you make this year that will end up increasing the extent of your joyful and fulfilling oversight of people or projects on the new earth?

4. Riches

I can't speak much to the currency of the eternal state, but I do have a verse that motivates me to expect that there will be various amounts of it awarded to God's people.

In the middle of a series of stories, parables, and lessons about our handling of money, Jesus said: "If then you have not been faithful in the unrighteous wealth, who will entrust to you the true riches?" (Luke 16:11). In this passage, Christ had just spoken of "unrighteous wealth" as the money of this earth that will eventually fail or become worthless (verse 9). Next, he compared earthly currency to a corresponding kind of money that won't fail—a true and eternal sort of currency that will last and always have buying power. This comes after he had just said, "One who is faithful in a very little is also faithful in much" (verse 10), which implies that the degree of faithfulness in the handling of *this* world's money will help determine the entrusted amount in the next.

Of course, in our new eternal home some things are specifically said to be free. Revelation 22:17 says that the water of life will be available to all the kingdom's inhabitants "without price." But based on that verse, I cannot say that there is no exchange of money for other goods and services. Again, I don't believe in celestial communism any more than I see any biblical allowance for earthly communism. And while I have no idea how commerce might work in the eternal state, I do know that there is a righteous and godly expression of it that can be engaged in now. Others have thoughtfully written on this topic,[6] but for now let me say that I can see how several expressions of buying, selling, business, and therefore money can reasonably exist in the next world. We'll have to wait and see.

5. Real Estate

And that brings us to real estate. If there will be buying, selling, business, and money in the next life, will there be ownership of personal property? Well, in a sense there is no personal property ownership now. Yes, a trust is given to those who have a legal stewardship of a set of coordinates on a map, but "the earth is the LORD's and the fullness thereof, the world and those who dwell therein" (Psalm 24:1).

Like our bodies now, we do have a kind of personal stewardship and "ownership" of them, but in fact our bodies are God's property. First Corinthians 6:19-20 makes that specific point: "You are not your own, for you were bought with a price." And yet the verse prior and the verse immediately following that statement refer to "your body" and one's "own body."

So to think, *Of course there will be no "private property" in the New Jerusalem because it is the Lord's place, not ours* is to overlook the kind of dual "ownership" that currently exists as it relates to our bodies and any plots of real estate that we may "own." It may be said that we own our bodies and properties, but only as stewards. And there is nothing sinful about talking about *our* bodies or *our* houses as long as we recognize that these are not absolute statements.

With that in view, consider the promise that followed the words directed to the apostles about their future responsibility in the kingdom. Jesus expanded the audience and said, "Everyone who has left houses or brothers or sisters or father or mother or children or lands, for my name's sake, will receive a hundredfold and will inherit eternal life" (Matthew 19:29). The context was treasure in heaven—that's what prompted Peter's question. After Jesus spoke of the job descriptions in our future home, he mentioned "houses" and "lands," promising "a hundredfold" for any sacrifices made in this life. That's enough for me to think that there will be various sizes and amounts of houses and lands allotted to those who have "stored them up" ahead of time. The deed process may be altogether different, and the clarity with which we think and understand that all things are truly owned by God may be different, but I take this verse to mean that there will be a stewardship over property—assigned in varying amounts to the citizens of the eternal kingdom.

6. Relationships

As difficult as it might be to explain, I should mention what is tucked between the words "houses" and "lands" in Matthew 19:29. You might have noticed the promise to those whose brothers, sisters, father, mother, or children have been in some way sacrificed for Christ and his priorities in this life. It is hard to envision how this might play out, but again, Jesus made the hundredfold promise.

We've likely already experienced that our commitment to Christ and his gospel costs us in the area of earthly relationships. Jesus was clear that sometimes our loyalty to the gospel will have a negative impact on our family relationships (Matthew 10:34-39). I know our modern version of Christianity doesn't like to talk about that. Sadly, many equate family and relational happiness and tranquility with godliness, but in the real world, following Christ and advancing his priorities in our lives, homes, and offices will strain and even break some relational ties. Godliness is always the goal, not trying to be liked or popular—even with our family members. But we can know that for every relationship that is strained or damaged in some way by our devotion to Christ, the Bible says that one day we will be rewarded with an exponential gain of family and friends. I am sure that on the new earth no one will lack in this department, but some, we understand from this passage, will have a rich abundance of fulfilling relationships.

THE ABSENCE OF COVETING

We can struggle with the thought of varying degrees of posses-sions, real estate, or relationships in the next life because we can't envision it without thinking it will provoke jealousy, envy, and cov-eting. Well, it won't. Sure, in this world it is hard to "rejoice with those who rejoice" (Romans 12:15). In our fallen state we naturally compare our assets and advantages to everyone else's. And when someone living next door has a better house, a better car, a better job, and a better income, we tend to resent it. But that's because of our fallen state. Our envy comes from our sinful flesh and is fueled by the tempter and his henchmen.

In the eternal state, we will all reside in glorified bodies. Our plotting spiritual enemy will be consigned to punishment, never to bother us again. We will sincerely and in every situation rejoice with those who have greater blessings than us.

For the Christian, I don't think this is too hard to imagine. If your church is like mine, the parking lot on Sunday is filled with a variety of cars—some cheap, some nice, and a few really nice ones. Inside, as we worship and study the Word, we have some people who are making minimum wage, some who are middle managers, and others who are CEOs and make crazy amounts of money. After church, people will return to houses of various sizes and values. Yet on our best day of the week, as we focus on God and his gracious sal-vation in Christ, sitting all together in subjection to his holy Word, none of those differences matter a whole lot. As we fellowship on the patio, discuss our lives, and pray together, we are all one body in Christ. We have moments of "heaven on earth" as we consider our equal footing before the cross. We know we are all sinners in need of grace. We know that none of us deserve anything. We accept one another, and on our best days, we don't envy others' things, we are not jealous of their jobs, and we don't covet their homes. That may not happen every Sunday we gather together, but we can be sure it will be the reality every single day when we live on the new earth.

CHAPTER 6

I'm Afraid I Might Sin My Way Out of Heaven

You may have heard the saying, "If you ever find a perfect church, don't join it—you'll mess it up!"

Of course, we know there are no perfect churches. And I hope we are all honest enough to admit that each of us is a flawed Christian in need of ongoing correction and spiritual growth. Even during the best seasons of our Christian lives we find ourselves stumbling into sin, saying things we shouldn't, and doing things we said we never would. So I guess the saying is true—if in fact we were to ever find a truly perfect church.

In the last chapter we considered that the Bible presents to us a perfect place, a new earth where righteousness dwells, a holy city where faultless Christ himself is enthroned. It is described to us as a community where "nothing unclean will ever enter it, nor anyone who does what is detestable or false" (Revelation 21:27). At first that sounds great, like the disgruntled churchgoer looking for his perfect church. But a little honest time sitting before the mirror of God's Word will likely send a chill up your spine—as you wonder how in the world you could ever fit in there.

If that thought has crossed your mind, you might have said to yourself, *I'm sure God will fix me up so I can fit right in.* But when the thought eventually bounces back, it can easily turn into a serious concern. How can this be? Will we be mere moral robots? Weren't Adam and Eve said to be in a perfect environment? What about Satan and the demons? They were in heaven, weren't they? They were in a perfect place with no tempters to tempt them, and yet they fell into sin and were cast out.

These are good questions, and we should take some time to thoughtfully and biblically consider them.

"FOREVER" DESCRIPTIONS

Before we consider how this might work, let's take a fresh look at what God says heaven will be like:

> No longer will there be anything accursed, but the throne of God and of the Lamb will be in it, and his servants will worship him. They will see his face, and his name will be on their foreheads. And night will be no more. They will need no light of lamp or sun, for the Lord God will be their light, and they will reign forever and ever (Revelation 22:3-5).

There is complete clarity that the people who will inhabit this new earth will be living in the presence of God and his gifts forever. "They will reign forever and ever"—there it is. The "they" in that verse are "his servants," those who "see his face," those who have his name "on their foreheads."

God said "the saints of the Most High shall receive the kingdom and possess the kingdom forever, forever and ever" (Daniel 7:18). He also said that they will continue to serve and obey him in this eternal state:

> The kingdom and the dominion and the greatness of the kingdoms under the whole heaven shall be given to the

people of the saints of the Most High; his kingdom shall
be an everlasting kingdom, and all dominions shall serve
and obey him (verse 27).

Jesus poetically illustrated the permanence of our future standing in the new earth by saying this to his followers in the church of
Philadelphia:

> The one who conquers, I will make him a pillar in the
> temple of my God. Never shall he go out of it, and I will
> write on him the name of my God, and the name of the
> city of my God, the new Jerusalem, which comes down
> from my God out of heaven, and my own new name
> (Revelation 3:12).

Again, we see this imagery of God "labeling" his people. He is
depicted as writing his name on the foreheads of his people (Revelation 22:4). He even labels them with his address—the New Jerusalem (Revelation 3:12). I don't write my name and address on the
paper napkin I get at the drive-thru fast food restaurant. I plan on
throwing it away. It is temporary. But like many people, I have
used my trusty label maker to tag several things that I own. I want
to make sure people know those labeled possessions belong to me.
They are not disposable. They are mine, for keeps.

I realize that for some, that is all they need—clear statements in
the Bible from God. Case closed. They will sleep well. They are the
kind who are content to know that if they push the right pedal, the
car will move. They don't need to know what transpires under
the hood. They are happy to flip the light switch and know that the
light will come on—no explanation needed. If that's you, I guess you
can move on to the next chapter. But for many of us, our hearts and
minds struggle with *how* this can be. If that's you too, then let's try
to understand the answer—beginning with God's work of justification and regeneration.

JUSTIFICATION AND REGENERATION

Justification is God's act of declaring us righteous when we repent of our sins and place our trust in Christ's redemptive work. Romans 4:5 says that he "justifies the ungodly," which is something Christians intuitively recognize because we have done nothing to earn this forgiveness. God has done the work and, as the verse goes on to say, our "faith is counted as righteousness." This gracious act of God—declaring sinners righteous—is also accompanied by the miraculous work we call *regeneration*, which simply means "to be reborn."

Though we all continue to battle the sinful impulses of our fallen flesh, the Bible says that the regenerating act of God's Spirit causes a transformation of our interior lives. We "were dead in...trespasses and sins," but now we have been made "alive together with Christ" (Ephesians 2:1, 5). In Christ we are "a new creation," for "the old has passed away" and "the new has come" (2 Corinthians 5:17). This new life is described as being raised up from the dead and being enabled to "walk in newness of life" (Romans 6:4). It is a "washing of regeneration and renewal of the Holy Spirit" (Titus 3:5). Something fundamental and profound has changed about who we now are. The Old Testament described this graciously granted interior change in this way:

> I will give them one heart, and a new spirit I will put within them. I will remove the heart of stone from their flesh and give them a heart of flesh, that they may walk in my statutes and keep my rules and obey them. And they shall be my people, and I will be their God (Ezekiel 11:19-20).

Plainly we see that Christians have been given a new capacity to love, serve, and obey God. This stands in stark contrast to the reason we need God's work of justification and regeneration—sin.

The sinful state in which we were born as children of Adam had so impacted our hearts that they were "not alive" to God. Like stone, they were incapable of truly loving, serving, or obeying God. As these dark verses in Romans 3 describe:

> …both Jews and Greeks, are under sin, as it is written: "None is righteous, no, not one; no one understands; no one seeks for God. All have turned aside; together they have become worthless; no one does good, not even one. Their throat is an open grave; they use their tongues to deceive. The venom of asps is under their lips. Their mouth is full of curses and bitterness. Their feet are swift to shed blood; in their paths are ruin and misery, and the way of peace they have not known. There is no fear of God before their eyes" (Romans 3:9-18).

We are now not only capable of choosing to sin, but we are now also capable—because of our reborn and transformed heart—to choose not to sin.

The difference between being "dead" in our trespasses and sins and being "alive in Christ" is huge. It includes the difference between our will (our decision-making capacities) *being bound* in sin—incapable of loving and serving God—and our will *being freed* to choose obedience, service to Christ, and a true love for God. This new freedom is not always exercised righteously, as any Christian can testify. But the radical change in our capacity is an important truth to note. We are now not only capable of choosing *to sin*, but we are now also capable—because of our reborn and transformed heart—to choose *not to sin*.

Our core desires have been changed. The "new self," as the Bible puts it, is able to be increasingly strengthened and matured as we learn and grow in our knowledge of God (Colossians 3:10). However, the reason those new, godly, core desires don't always prevail in our decision making is threefold: the world, the flesh, and the devil.

THE WORLD AND ITS REPLACEMENT

In this chapter, the first passage I referenced about our eternal home begins with the words "no longer will there be anything accursed" (Revelation 22:3). The context indicates that this is a statement about the physical environment in which we will live. Way back since Genesis 3, the world has been under a curse imposed by God. The fabric of the universe is corrupt as a result of the just sentence of God when Adam and Eve sinned. Nothing works quite the way it is supposed to. From weather patterns that destroy cities to the chemistry in our brains that causes headaches, everything— down to the molecular level of creation—is echoing the rebellion that our first parents chose to participate in.

In God's mercy, the physical world is not as bad off as it could be. The glory and beauty of God can still be recognized in its reflection. The function of many aspects of our fallen world still yield good and profitable results. Yet the Bible says there is something so much better coming.

> The creation waits with eager longing for the revealing of the sons of God. For the creation was subjected to futility, not willingly, but because of him who subjected it, in hope that the creation itself will be set free from its bondage to corruption and obtain the freedom of the glory of the children of God (Romans 8:19-21).

This "bondage to corruption" will be reversed. The new earth will have no trace of the curse of Genesis 3. All that now impedes our godly aspirations and virtuous determinations will then aid them. The world, down to the molecular structure of creation, will assist us in doing what is righteous.

That may be a kind of obstruction to your consistent godliness that you don't think of often, but I assume you do frequently get frustrated over the way the fallen people of this world work to hinder your godly decisions. Every Christian's resolve to live in faithful obedience to God can testify to the truth of 2 Timothy 3:12-13: "Indeed, all who desire to live a godly life in Christ Jesus will be persecuted, while evil people and impostors will go on from bad to worse, deceiving and being deceived."

As Jesus said,

> If the world hates you, know that it has hated me before it hated you. If you were of the world, the world would love you as its own; but because you are not of the world, but I chose you out of the world, therefore the world hates you. Remember the word that I said to you: "A servant is not greater than his master." If they persecuted me, they will also persecute you (John 15:18-20).

The anti-Christian culture of our world may seem to be worse than ever, but the Bible and history both attest that it has always been this way. Yes, it will continue to get worse, but since Genesis 3 it has never been good. The sinful majority is the norm, and much of our fight to do what the Bible and our core desires are directing us to do is hampered by the pressure of the lost people around us.

"But according to his promise we are waiting for new heavens and a new earth in which righteousness dwells" (2 Peter 3:13). This is the report on the coming world: righteousness! It will be inhabited only by people made righteous and living righteously. It will be a metropolis of redeemed people with new hearts, people who walk in God's statues and are careful to obey his rules (Ezekiel 36:26-27).

God has promised that "nothing unclean will ever enter it, nor anyone who does what is detestable or false, but only those who are written in the Lamb's book of life" (Revelation 21:27). The cursed world and rebellious people will no longer be a threat to your continued faithfulness.

THE FLESH AND GLORIFICATION

I assume you have experienced times of being as isolated as possible from the influence of the world's rebellious culture—perhaps while on a hike, or at a retreat, or during a quiet hour of communion with God in an insulated prayer closet. And maybe in that solitary setting your health, the weather, and the immediate environment around you was also as perfect as it can be this side of eternity. Yet I am sure you found that sinful thoughts, selfish desires, and unrighteous attitudes still interrupted what you had hoped would be a perfectly holy afternoon. These are the impulses of the flesh. Scripture tells us that even for growing Christians the "desires of the flesh are against the Spirit, and the desires of the Spirit are against the flesh, for these are opposed to each other, to keep you from doing the things you want to do" (Galatians 5:17).

How frustrating that an enemy of our righteousness is hardwired into the very fabric of our humanity! If you were to picture yourself as a computer (as silly as this may sound), your system software was replaced when you were justified and regenerated. You are a new person in Christ. You, the real you, has been completely remade to spiritually interface with God and have fellowship with him. You have been enabled to love him, serve him, and obey him. But for now, your hardware remains the same. Same old parts—same circuits, same hard drive, same motherboard. And that is where the real problem lies.

Not only does this new software work in a sluggish fashion within this old hardware, but the hardware contains its own kind of software called firmware. The code programmed in this firmware has a very intrusive effect on how that new operating system is going to function. As a Christian you have a new heart that, at its core, beats in sync with God's truth and Christ's righteous standards. Deep down you want to love and serve God, regardless of what the world pressures you to do. But the impulse from your permanently encoded hardware, called your flesh, is always fighting against you. God says that for now you have to be aware and hold back from fulfilling these "passions of the flesh, which wage war against your soul" (1 Peter 2:11).

In the New Jerusalem, this will no longer be a problem. Your new software, created by God's Spirit to exclusively bring glory and honor to Christ through every facet of your personality, will have a freshly remanufactured hardware box with a flawless hard drive, pristine circuits, and a motherboard filled with a God-honoring, righteous code. From your operating system to your hardware to the firmware that directs its functions, it will be "all systems go" for righteous living! In the same way that everything about Christ's resurrected body functions righteously, and all of its instincts, urges, and inclinations are godly, so your future body will be. He has promised to "transform our lowly body to be like his glorious body, by the power that enables him even to subject all things to himself" (Philippians 3:21).

God calls this celebrated graduation our glorification. And it is guaranteed for every Christian. Those whom the Lord justifies, he also glorifies (Romans 8:30). It will be a completion of the personal transformation intended by God when he saved us. In the words of one theologian, the doctrine of glorification is the

> complete and final redemption of the whole person when in the integrity of body and spirit the people of God will be conformed to the image of the risen, exalted, and glorified Redeemer, when the very body of their humiliation will be conformed to the body of Christ's glory.[1]

THE DEVIL AND THE LAKE OF FIRE

We have a spiritual enemy who is most frequently called by the name *Satan*, which means "adversary." And he is certainly active in that pursuit. He and his henchmen oppose our sanctification by every means possible. The watchword for the present age is this:

> Be sober-minded; be watchful. Your adversary the devil prowls around like a roaring lion, seeking someone to devour. Resist him, firm in your faith, knowing that the same kinds of suffering are being experienced by your brotherhood throughout the world (1 Peter 5:8-9).

He will work against our resolve to live righteously by lying to us (John 8:44), by tempting us (1 Thessalonians 3:5), by accusing us (Revelation 12:10), by counterfeiting the truth (2 Corinthians 11:14), and by slandering us (1 Timothy 5:14-15), just to name a few of the insidious schemes he employs (Ephesians 6:11). A biblical study of the names describing our spiritual enemy can open our eyes to the variety of ways he actively seeks to set back our walk with Christ.[2] He is so good at what he does, I am sure we will look back from heaven's perspective and see, with sober clarity, how often he and his underlings were behind the detours and stumbling in our Christian life.

The good news is that a day is coming when he will never harass anyone again. When we arrive at our final destination, none of his invisible stirrings to do wrong will be possible. The Bible promises that the devil, who has worked so hard to tempt and deceive, will be "thrown into the lake of fire and sulfur where the beast and the false prophet were, and they will be tormented day and night forever and ever" (Revelation 20:10). There will be no escape from that point forward. God will remand Satan to *never* harass his creation again.

This is all made possible by the victorious work of Jesus Christ. First John 3:8 reminds us that "the reason the Son of God appeared was to destroy the works of the devil" (1 John 3:8). And he has already paid the price to make his doom sure. With a word, as Martin Luther poetically wrote, his harassment will end:

> And tho' this world, with devils filled,
>   Should threaten to undo us,
> We will not fear, for God hath willed
>   His truth to triumph thro' us;
> The prince of Darkness grim,
>   We tremble not for him;
> His rage we can endure,
>   or lo, his doom is sure,
> One little word shall fell him.[3]

It is old language, but good. Satan will be "felled" like a giant tree in the woods. Cut low and cut down—finally and for sure. It is reported that Luther had the word *liar* in mind when he spoke of that "one little word."[4] Surely he is, and God will, with the ease of speaking a word, consign him to his rightful place away from his new creation (2 Peter 3:5-7). What a day of victory and relief that will be for God's children!

We have much to look forward to—namely, a life in eternity free from those things that constrain and oppose righteousness. In the end, the desires of our regenerate hearts to perfectly and faithfully love and serve Christ will not be opposed in the slightest or impeded in any way by the world, the flesh, or the devil.

WHAT ABOUT ADAM AND EVE?

The Bible is symmetrically bookended by four chapters, two on each side, that give us a picture of two sinless worlds. One tells us of the Garden of Eden—with perfectly righteous people enjoying unhindered fellowship with God. The other shows us the New Jerusalem—with perfectly righteous people enjoying unhindered fellowship with God. When the Lord introduces the holy city, he will say, "It is done! I am the Alpha and the Omega, the beginning and the end" (Revelation 21:6).

The question is, how do we know we won't have another Genesis 3 episode following Revelation 21 and 22? After all, Adam and Eve lived in a flawless world, in bodies untainted by the curse and sin.

Based on where we've been in this chapter, our first reaction might be, "They had a tempter tempting them and we won't." That's true. And it is a big difference, but theologians have had to also conclude that there was something different about the capacities of Adam and Eve as compared to the capacities glorified individuals will have in the New Jerusalem—at least as it relates to sin. In their innocent state, Adam and Eve did not have the propensity to sin as people do now, but they also did not have the kind of union with God that we will have in our glorified state. Though the Bible does not describe the details of this difference, the philosophical minds of deep theologians, from Augustine to Jonathan Edwards, have concluded that the innocent state of Adam and Eve had a vulnerability that those united with Christ in eternity will not have.

In short, our freedom in the New Jerusalem will be as free and nonrobotic as Adam and Eve's, but our ability or capacity to sin will be absent. We will no more choose to sin than a dog would choose to be a dolphin. This is not because we won't have the ability to make free choices, but because we've lived through a "post-innocent" reality, and because of the regenerating work of God's Spirit in our hearts and his restorative work in our bodies, we can conclude that there will be absolutely no enticement to sin.

THE MILLENNIUM TRIAL

My reference to living through "post-innocent" reality is, I believe, the reason for an otherwise odd reference to a season of tempting by Satan at the end of the millennium.

The millennium, described in Revelation 20, is a period of 1,000 years, which will begin after the return of Christ in the battle of Armageddon—his return will take place following the seven years of "great tribulation." This 1,000 years will be a time of specific fulfillment of God's promises to the descendants of Abraham.[5] There will be a very large number of people in glorified bodies ruling and reigning with Christ during this period—saved people who died and are resurrected before this 1,000 years begins.[6] But there will also be people in unglorified bodies, those who placed their trust in Christ and lived through the Tribulation. These people, according to the Old Testament promises, will marry, have children, and live long and prosperous lives (Isaiah 65:19-25).

The Bible tells us that during the millennium, Satan will be confined and then later released.

> Then I saw an angel coming down from heaven, holding in his hand the key to the bottomless pit and a great chain. And he seized the dragon, that ancient serpent, who is the devil and Satan, and bound him for a thousand years, and threw him into the pit, and shut it and sealed it over him, so that he might not deceive the nations any longer, until the thousand years were ended. After that he must be released for a little while (Revelation 20:1-3).

During the 1,000 years of prosperity a lot of people will be born who have never experienced anything but Christ and his glorified saints ruling and reigning over a spiritually tranquil world. But that "innocence" will be tested. As sad as this "release for a short while" is, it seems to be necessary to put before these people who know nothing but Christ's lordship. Here is how it is described:

> When the thousand years are ended, Satan will be released from his prison and will come out to deceive the

nations that are at the four corners of the earth, Gog and Magog, to gather them for battle; their number is like the sand of the sea. And they marched up over the broad plain of the earth and surrounded the camp of the saints and the beloved city, but fire came down from heaven and consumed them, and the devil who had deceived them was thrown into the lake of fire and sulfur where the beast and the false prophet were, and they will be tormented day and night forever and ever (verses 7-10).

Like the tree of the knowledge of good and evil in the Garden, or the call of the gospel against the backdrop of our sinful culture, these "innocents" will have right and wrong set before them—the Lord and his faithful leadership, or the deceiver's temptation to rebel. Unfortunately, scores of people, we are told, will fall.

God will apparently populate the new earth only with those who are sealed in their righteous standing and have lived through a post-innocent reality.

WHAT ABOUT SATAN AND THE DEMONS?

Last, we are left with the question of how a sinless angel fell into sin without an external tempter. This is a fall into sin we are told little about.

Isaiah 14 and Ezekiel 28 speak of the sinful corruption of the Old Testament rulers of Babylon and Tyre, but both passages, in obvious ways, pull back the curtain on the history of the fall of the ultimate power behind every sinful leader—Satan himself. God describes him this way:

You were the signet of perfection, full of wisdom and perfect in beauty. You were in Eden, the garden of God; every precious stone was your covering, sardius, topaz, and diamond, beryl, onyx, and jasper, sapphire, emerald, and carbuncle; and crafted in gold were your settings and your engravings. On the day that you were created they were prepared. You were an anointed guardian cherub. I placed you; you were on the holy mountain of God; in the midst of the stones of fire you walked. You were blameless in your ways from the day you were created, till unrighteousness was found in you (Ezekiel 28:12-15).

This "blameless" "signet of perfection" was suddenly filled with unrighteousness. A brief explanation follows: "Your heart was proud because of your beauty; you corrupted your wisdom for the sake of your splendor" (verse 17). The disclosure of this tragic event is expanded in Isaiah.

You said in your heart, "I will ascend to heaven; above the stars of God I will set my throne on high; I will sit on the mount of assembly in the far reaches of the north; I will ascend above the heights of the clouds; I will make myself like the Most High" (Isaiah 14:13-14).

His prideful self-exaltation was backed by a third of the angelic host:

Another sign appeared in heaven: behold, a great red dragon, with seven heads and ten horns, and on his heads seven diadems. His tail swept down a third of the stars of heaven and cast them to the earth. And the dragon stood before the woman who was about to give birth, so that when she bore her child he might devour it (Revelation 12:3-4).

There is no doubt in the context about his identity:

The great dragon was thrown down, that ancient serpent, who is called the devil and Satan, the deceiver of the

> whole world—he was thrown down to the earth, and
> his angels were thrown down with him (Revelation 12:9).

As unsettling as it might be to consider that perfectly upright beings, in a perfectly righteous environment, and in the presence of a perfectly holy God, suddenly became sinners, this scenario is promised to be unrepeatable. As we have seen, when we are perfected in God's presence and in our new eternal home, God has guaranteed our status will be unending. This one-time disruption to the experience by innocent angelic beings is not even repeatable for them. The crisis of going through this post-innocent reality has forever changed their status and description in the Bible. Like the crisis in the Garden, or the calamity at the end of the millennium, the angels' futures are set. We know this because God refers to those who did not rebel as his "elect angels" (1 Timothy 5:21). In contrast, those who did rebel are now called the devil's angels (Matthew 25:41).

In God's wise plan, and to the demonstration of his matchless mercy and grace, allowing sinful musings to enter the mind of a high-ranking angelic being has resulted in an experience of testing for every created being in the universe. From angels witnessing the self-promotion of one of their own, and Eve heeding the enticement of the serpent, to the call of repentance, which every generation since has heard and felt, the choice of life and death has been laid before us all (Deuteronomy 30:19). And for those of us who have, by God's grace, been drawn to cling to the cross of Christ, we have the confidence of an eternity without sin, temptation, or failure. What a relief and assurance this should be for us.

Perhaps an excerpt from Charles Wesley's poetry captures best the joy, security, and gratitude that I hope will settle into your heart and mind as you anticipate your future home.

> Savior of sinful men,
>   Thy goodness we proclaim,

Which brings us here to meet again,
    And triumph in Thy name!
Thy mighty name hath been
    Our refuge and our tower,
Hath saved us from the world, and sin,
    And all the' accuser's power.
Through calumny, and pain,
    Through a long vale of woe,
Far from the poisonous sons of men,
    To purer worlds we go:
We shall from Sodom flee,
    When perfected in love,
And haste to better company,
    Who wait for us above.
The saints of ancient days,
    We shall with them sit down,
Who fought the fight, and run the race,
    And then received the crown;
Who first severely tried,
    And exercised beneath,
Broke through the world, with Christ their guide,
    And more than conquer'd death.
Oh! what a mighty change
    Shall Jesu's sufferers know,
While o'er the happy plains we range,
    Incapable of woe!
No ill-requited love
    Shall there our spirits wound,
No base ingratitude above,
    No sin in heaven is found.[7]

CHAPTER 7

There Is No Hell

B y far the most familiar piece from the famous French sculptor Auguste Rodin is undoubtedly the work that came to be known as *The Thinker.* I'm sure you know the one I am referring to. He's that contemplative guy on a rock (in desperate need of some clothing) looking down, with his chin resting on the back of his hand. You can visit the original piece at a museum in Paris, but if you happen to have a lot of books in your personal library you may have a miniature copy of this sculpture serving as a bookend on one of your shelves.

These days, depictions of this statue are everywhere. I've seen it portrayed in television commercials, on billboards, and in editorial cartoons on news sites. Most frequently, however, this familiar figure is found on college and university brochures and web pages representing their departments of philosophy. It seems appropriate enough—one would have to think pretty hard and spend hours in deep thought and deliberation to figure out the teachings of Aristotle, Descartes, or Camus. But actually, when Rodin crafted this piece more than 100 years ago, he designed it to make us ponder theology, not philosophy.

Rodin called his sculpture *The Poet,* not *The Thinker.* And the poet he was referring to was the fourteenth-century Italian poet Dante Alighieri, who authored the epic work entitled *Inferno* (the Italian word for *hell*). Rodin designed this figure as part of an ensemble, with the poet pensively and reflectively looking down at a set of gates that are called *The Gates of Hell*. Next time you see a detailed replica, look closely at *The Poet*'s face—you'll notice he is not thinking happy thoughts. Knowing the context and meaning of this work will certainly enable you to recognize his pained and sober expression as he ponders the tragedy of lost people.

The scene is all the more poignant if you've ever read Dante's depiction of those gates. He describes them as having the following inscription written above their entrance:

> Through me the way to the Infernal City;
> Through me the way to eternal sadness;
> Through me the way to the lost people.
> Justice moved my Supreme Maker;
> I was shaped by Divine Power, by Highest Wisdom,
>   and by Primal Love.
> Before me, nothing was created that is not eternal;
> And eternal I endure.
> Forsake all hope, all you that enter here.[1]

Now, take in for a moment what Rodin wanted us to experience as we view the pensive poet contemplating the fate of lost men and women shuffling their way into their final abode.

This, I understand, is hard to take in. It is difficult now, and it was understood to be a difficult doctrine when Dante penned those words in the fourteenth century. Notice the narrative that picks up after the sign is read:

> These were the words, with their dark color, that I saw
> written above the gate, at which I said: "Master, their

meaning, to me, is hard." And he replied to me, as one
who knows: "Here, all uncertainty must be left behind:
all cowardice must be dead."[2]

Yes, talking, writing, or reading about the doctrine of hell is not
for cowards. The contents of these next few chapters are difficult to
take in. But our guide is not a French sculptor or an Italian poet.
Our guide must be none other than the Lord Jesus Christ, who in
the greatest expression of love came to give his life as a ransom for
many. Jesus has spoken on this topic, as has the entirety of the Bible.
We must boldly resolve to let God himself inform us about what lies
beyond for those who refuse to cling to the grace and forgiveness
abundantly provided to us in Christ.

A TIME TO WEEP

I can only imagine that many will be tempted to skip these chapters because of the current climate of our society. Our culture has
reached a place where any prospects of a negative reality is attacked
as heresy. It used to be that difficult doctrines like this were quietly
overlooked. Then they were purposely swept under the carpet. But
now if you believe the things in the Bible that have sharp edges, you
are labeled a hate-monger and an evil person.

I can appreciate our preference for happy texts (as Pollyanna put
it). I know we'd rather laugh than cry. I can identify with wanting
only the good news and not the bad. But if my mail carrier sat at
the end of people's driveways sorting the "good mail" from the "bad
mail," the "happy letters" from the "sad letters," the people on that
route would have him fired. Worse than filtering out the teaching
on hell, today's Christian "mail carriers" are ready to write letters of
complaint on our behalf to God for anything they find in his com-
munication that smacks of negativity.

> *We cannot allow our emotional reactions to*
> *biblical truth to serve as a test of whether*
> *or not certain teachings are true.*

Well, as the Bible says, there is a time to laugh *and* a time to weep; a time to dance *but also* a time to mourn (Ecclesiastes 3:4). If you have no time to weep or mourn over the hard truths of the Bible, or you, like so many, are tempted to avoid the painful doctrines at all costs, then at least you should recognize that you've created a Bible and a God of your own making. We cannot allow our emotional reactions to biblical truth to serve as a test of whether or not certain teachings are true.

That may seem logical enough—as rational as knowing that I cannot *pretend* I didn't get a letter that I didn't happen to like. But this is precisely what many of today's so-called Christian leaders advocate. For example, here's an excerpt from a recent best-seller on the topic:

> I've written this book for all those, everywhere, who have heard some version of the Jesus story that caused their pulse rate to rise, their stomach to churn, and their heart to utter those resolute words, "I would never be a part of that." You are not alone. There are millions of us. This love compels us to question some of the dominant stories that are being told as the Jesus story. A staggering number of people have been taught that a select few Christians will spend forever in a peaceful, joyous place called heaven, while the rest of humanity spends forever in torment and punishment in hell with no chance for anything better. It's been clearly communicated to many that this belief is a central truth of the Christian faith and to reject it is, in essence, to reject Jesus. This is misguided and toxic and ultimately subverts the contagious

spread of Jesus's message of love, peace, forgiveness, and
joy that our world desperately needs to hear.[3]

Biblically speaking, that is not the message the world *needs* to
hear. But it is unquestionably the message they *want* to hear. We
would like all the laughing and dancing without any of the weeping and mourning. But the Bible doesn't leave us with that option—
reality will engender both. We are, as I stated earlier in this book, on
a sinking ship called *humanity*. Our sins have drilled holes in the
hull. The vessel is already listing hard and about to go under. But
God has equipped this ship with a rescue boat. Christ is the captain of that boat, and he gave his life to pay the price to deliver us. If
we don't see the peril we are in and accept the sobering diagnosis of
our plight, if we don't run in faith and repentance to the only hope
of our salvation, then we haven't taken the problem seriously. We
clearly haven't contemplated the pending consequences of rejecting
God's gracious means of deliverance.

NOTHING NEW

It may seem that we are at an all-time high when it comes to the
impatience and intolerance regarding the hard truths about the doctrine of divine punishment, but this is nothing new. Even in biblical
times people worked overtime to suppress the witness of creation,
their consciences, and the preaching of repentance. They falsely rea-
soned that God would not punish their unrepentant hearts for their
sins. Psalm 10:11 diagnoses an enduring perspective from the heart
that refuses to repent: "God has forgotten, he has hidden his face,
he will never see it." Or even the more common thought that, "God
may see it, but he would never discipline me for it; I'm sure he is like
me in the values he holds":

> For you hate discipline, and you cast my words behind
> you. If you see a thief, you are pleased with him, and you

keep company with adulterers. "You give your mouth free rein for evil, and your tongue frames deceit. You sit and speak against your brother; you slander your own mother's son. These things you have done, and I have been silent; you thought that I was one like yourself. But now I rebuke you and lay the charge before you" (Psalm 50:17-21).

We dare not foolishly suppose that God conforms his rules to the likings of our hearts—we cannot assume he is just like us! Instead, we must carefully conform our hearts and minds to God's revealed rules. Yet so many have worked hard to avoid what God has clearly revealed.

For example, Hinduism denies the reality of a place of divine punishment for sinners. It teaches that "there is no external hell, nor is there a Satan."[4]

Hindus believe, like so many in Western culture, that hell is on earth. Through a series of reincarnations, there may be "hellish states of mind and woeful births for those who think and act wrongfully," but this is all a temporary condition that springs from within yourself.[5] There is not accountability to a creator.

Buddhism, does speak of a version of hell inhabited by demons, but insists that when it comes to human beings, hell is simply "a name for painful feelings."[6] In fact, Buddhism teaches that "we create our own hell" and are "responsible for our own happiness and misery."[7] Again, with the teaching of karma and reincarnation, there is no accountability to a personal creator.

Mary Baker Eddy, the founder of Christian Science, spoke often of her disdain for the doctrine of hell. She, like so many today, taught that "no final judgment awaits mortals, for the judgment-day of wisdom comes hourly and continually."[8] "Sin makes its own hell, and goodness its own heaven."[9]

Both Jehovah's Witnesses and Seventh-Day Adventists have

advocated for decades the increasingly popular thought that the unrepentant simply cease to exist when they die physically. Adventist doctrine teaches that "the wages of sin is *death,* not eternal life in hell."[10] The Jehovah's Witnesses's website likewise states, "the idea that he would punish people in hellfire is contrary to the Bible's teaching that 'God is love.'"[11]

These groups, like a growing number of supposedly evangelical Christians, tell us there can be no possible compatibility between a loving God and a place called hell.

LOVE WARNS!

Let's evaluate that definition of love. After all, this is the common refrain: "If God loves, there would be no such place as hell." The best-selling book I quoted earlier that wants to twist, contort, or extract anything from the pages of the Bible that makes one's pulse race or stomach churn is entitled *Love Wins.* But according to Scripture, *love warns!* This was the assessment of Christ, the apostles, and every other prophetic figure in the Bible. Consider the teaching of the one preacher Jesus praised above all others—John the Baptist. Of him, Christ said, "none is greater" (Luke 7:28). But I'm pretty sure his preaching would be criticized, scolded, and banned by most of today's best-selling religious authors. Here is a dose of the preaching from the prophet Jesus so highly valued. Picture him as you read his words, envision him behind the pulpit of the church in your town. See him in modern clothing, standing on the platform of your church, passionately delivering these warnings:

> He said therefore to the crowds that came out to be baptized by him, "You brood of vipers! Who warned you to flee from the wrath to come? Bear fruits in keeping with repentance. And do not begin to say to yourselves, 'We have Abraham as our father.' For I tell you, God is

able from these stones to raise up children for Abraham. Even now the axe is laid to the root of the trees. Every tree therefore that does not bear good fruit is cut down and thrown into the fire."

And the crowds asked him, "What then shall we do?" And he answered them, "Whoever has two tunics is to share with him who has none, and whoever has food is to do likewise." Tax collectors also came to be baptized and said to him, "Teacher, what shall we do?" And he said to them, "Collect no more than you are authorized to do." Soldiers also asked him, "And we, what shall we do?" And he said to them, "Do not extort money from anyone by threats or by false accusation, and be content with your wages."

As the people were in expectation, and all were questioning in their hearts concerning John, whether he might be the Christ, John answered them all, saying, "I baptize you with water, but he who is mightier than I is coming, the strap of whose sandals I am not worthy to untie. He will baptize you with the Holy Spirit and fire. His winnowing fork is in his hand, to clear his threshing floor and to gather the wheat into his barn, but the chaff he will burn with unquenchable fire." So with many other exhortations he preached good news to the people (Luke 3:7-18).

I realize that was a long quotation, and you may have read it before, but I didn't want to leave out anything that would help to give you a sense of the emphasis, urgency, as well as the description that God gives this preaching through Luke. Namely, that this was the "good news" (verse 18). He was preaching "good news"! The news that there was a way of escape from the coming penalty of sin is called *good*. It is actually the best news of all! Knowing that there is a call of repentance and trust in the Messiah, which opens to us the undeserved mercy of God's forgiveness, is indeed good news.

The love of God can never be understood or appreciated as the incredible good news that it is, unless we see that it is the gracious solution to the very bad news of sin and judgment. All this "hellfire" preaching was looked upon favorably by Jesus, for he wants sinners to see their great need and come to the provided source of salvation.

These warnings are essential. We cannot have gospel preaching (that is, "good news messages") *without* the admonition that we live our lives before the Creator, and all possess the human dignity of being accountable to him. This preaching is in fact the most loving preaching possible because it speaks the truth about our problem. This message is not hateful, it is compassionate. To be warned that drilling holes into the hull of our lives is sinking this ship is the first step in pointing us to the remedy. The teaching and preaching of divine judgment may initially be harsh news in the ears of sinners, but it is certainly necessary for understanding the good news!

THE TEACHING OF JESUS

If you were to ask people to take a few minutes to close their eyes and to imagine the Jesus Christ of history, they would likely picture a pretty chill guy. They would probably envision him teaching nice things, hugging children, encouraging his pals to be at peace, and offering words of encouragement and comfort to strangers. What a jarring wake-up call it would be if, with their eyes still closed, you started reading some of the recorded words of Christ. Words that Jesus spoke to his friends, such as,

> I tell you, my friends, do not fear those who kill the body, and after that have nothing more that they can do. But I will warn you whom to fear: fear him who, after he has killed, has authority to cast into hell. Yes, I tell you, fear him! (Luke 12:4-5).

Churchgoers who say, "No one should scare people into believing the gospel" would bristle at those words.

What about those who imagine Jesus as someone who wouldn't hurt a fly? You could continue reading just a little further in the same passage, where Jesus says, "I came to cast fire on the earth, and would that it were already kindled" (verse 49). Next, think of the response you would get as you read Christ's forecast of the coming fiery judgment:

> Just as the weeds are gathered and burned with fire, so will it be at the end of the age. The Son of Man will send his angels, and they will gather out of his kingdom all causes of sin and all law-breakers, and throw them into the fiery furnace. In that place there will be weeping and gnashing of teeth (Matthew 13:40-42).

And, lest anyone think that analogy of burning weeds in the fire referred to some kind of "extinguishing termination" to people's existence, Jesus said, "It is better for you to enter the kingdom of God with one eye than with two eyes to be thrown into hell, 'where their worm does not die and the fire is not quenched'" (Mark 9:47-48). And then Jesus provided further elaboration on this judgment when he spoke of a former rich man who

> died and was carried by the angels to Abraham's side. The rich man also died and was buried, and in Hades, being in torment, he lifted up his eyes and saw Abraham far off and Lazarus at his side. And he called out, "Father Abraham, have mercy on me, and send Lazarus to dip the end of his finger in water and cool my tongue, for I am in anguish in this flame" (Luke 16:22-24).

Just this brief reading of the historic words of Jesus would quickly shatter the modern myth of a meek and mild Jesus who possesses some version of love that would never conceive of sinners entering a literal place of judgment for their sins. The only thing left for incredulous people who will not accept this historic record of Jesus is to attack the historicity of the biblical record. But, in fact, this will get the honest student of history nowhere, as so many others have handily addressed.[12]

Talk about quickening pulse and a churning stomach! We don't need a congregation of uptight Bible thumpers preaching at us; all we need to do is to pick up our Bibles and read what Jesus said. Jesus, as honest theologians have always reminded us, gives us the strongest and clearest teaching on the doctrine of eternal punishment. This makes sense, knowing he had certainly witnessed the tragic reality of postmortem judgment prior to his incarnation. Thoughtfully consider the words of nineteenth-century theologian William Shedd:

> The strongest support of the doctrine of endless punishment is the teaching of Christ, the Redeemer of man. Though the doctrine is plainly taught in the Pauline epistles and other parts of Scripture, yet without the explicit and reiterated statements of God incarnate, it is doubtful whether so awful a truth would have had such a conspicuous place as it always has had in the creed of Christendom. If, in spite of that large mass of positive and solemn threatening of everlasting punishment from the lips of Jesus Christ which is recorded in the four gospels, the attempt has nevertheless been made to prove that the tenet is not an integral part of the Christian system, we may be certain that had this portion of revelation been wanting, this attempt would have been much more frequent and much more successful.[13]

JUDGMENT

I cannot deny that from our earthly perspective the concept of a celestial tribunal where judgment is dispensed on human beings is an unpleasant and difficult thought—that is, until we think through the rationale of why human courtrooms exist. God is presented to us in the Bible as a God of justice. We know this biblically and intuitively. We can affirm with Abraham the obvious answer to his rhetorical question, "Shall not the Judge of all the earth do what is just?" (Genesis 18:25). And the lyrics of an Old Testament worship song affirm what we instinctively know: "Righteousness and justice are the foundation of your throne" (Psalm 89:14).

God is righteous and just. He does what is right and he is concerned about what is appropriate, equitable, and fair. We want these traits in a judge. Suppose I were to campaign for the office of superior court judge in your county. Let's say I campaigned on the virtue of my character. I want the entire county to know that I am a nice, kind, and loving person. So, I choose as my campaign slogan "Mike Fabarez, the loving judge." I then travel the county giving my campaign speeches. I talk about how lenient and charitable I am. I continue to talk about how "love will always win out" in my courtroom. In every case set before me, I will let my love be clearly seen. I speak of how much I hate judgment. I tell the crowds at my rallies that I believe first and foremost in the goodness of every man and woman. In trying to garner your vote, I continually promise that I will see to it that no one is punished, and not a single criminal will be subject to any unpleasant consequences for their crimes. I am careful to end all my speeches with the chant "Vote for me, all go free! Vote for me, all go free!"

I wonder how many votes I would receive from the people in your neighborhood. Would I get your vote? I think not.

I'm sure you want your county judges to be decent, loving, and kind people. You would want them to love their spouses and their children. You would want them to be nice people. You would hope that they would be considerate, thoughtful, and fair in how they hear and adjudicate the people standing trial before them. But you would also want them to be just. You and your neighbors would want your county judges to uphold the law. You would want judges who judge righteously according to the rules.

Wouldn't we have the same expectation of God? He, of course, is loving and also perfectly equitable, always correct and appropriate in his compensation of every moral breach and transgression of the law. God will never pervert justice (Job 34:12). He "does no injustice" (Zephaniah 3:5). It is said of Christ that "in righteousness he judges" (Revelation 19:11). And God "has fixed a day on which he will judge the world in righteousness" (Acts 17:31).

THE JUDGMENT OF THE CROSS

That last verse I quoted is preceded by a call to repent. Here's the whole context:

> The times of ignorance God overlooked, but now he commands all people everywhere to repent, because he has fixed a day on which he will judge the world in righteousness by a man whom he has appointed; and of this he has given assurance to all by raising him from the dead (Acts 17:30-31).

An introspective reading of those verses on God's justice in the previous section should lead us all to think, *Without the cross, we are all sunk!* That is true. Absolutely! If God is always perfectly equitable and always appropriate in his compensation of every moral breach and transgression of the law, then a truthful run through the memory of our sins just this past week would leave us hopeless—that is, without Christ and his cross.

If every sin is compensated and justly responded to by a perfectly holy God; and Christ will one day judge every thought, word, and deed that falls short of his righteous standard; then we all stand condemned. Well, we *would* stand condemned were it not for the dreadful yet amazing drama that played out on the cross of Christ.

Again, another lengthy quote from Scripture, but please read it thoughtfully, as though you were reading it for the first time:

> Now we know that whatever the law says it speaks to those who are under the law, so that every mouth may be stopped, and the whole world may be held accountable to God. For by works of the law no human being will be justified in his sight, since through the law comes knowledge of sin.
>
> But now the righteousness of God has been manifested apart from the law, although the Law and the Prophets bear witness to it—the righteousness of God through faith in Jesus Christ for all who believe. For there is no distinction: for all have sinned and fall short of the glory of God, and are justified by his grace as a gift, through the redemption that is in Christ Jesus, whom God put forward as a propitiation by his blood, to be received by faith. This was to show God's righteousness, because in his divine forbearance he had passed over former sins (Romans 3:19-25).

The suffering of Christ on the cross as a "propitiation," or righteous settlement of our debt before God, is the ultimate expression of God's justice. The Lord maintains his perfect justice of compensating for every sinful infraction, while being motivated by his incredible love to have his own Son assume the penalty for us. "For our sake he made him to be sin who knew no sin, so that in him we might become the righteousness of God" (2 Corinthians 5:21). We are declared holy, having faultless righteousness credited to us through faith, because Jesus was impartially treated as though he had committed every one of our moral breaches and transgressions.

It is ironic that the centerpiece of Christian theology can remain in view (Christ's death on a cross) when so many have now chosen to deny God's just punishment of sin. We should be reminded of the reality of hell every time we look to the cross, for the cross is the absorption of the full impact of God's punishment for those of us who have reached out for the benefit made possible by Christ's death. To deny the biblical truth of a God who judges sin, while affirming his holiness, the wickedness of sin, and the suffering and sacrifice of Jesus on the cross cannot logically add up. Hell is an integral part of these central theological truths.[14]

Many people who express their belief in God miss this logical contradiction. But, as you might imagine, the leaders of the modern "Christian" movement who dismiss the doctrine of hell are working to redefine all these truths. God's holiness is being understood in sentimental ways. Sin has been put on a sliding scale, determined by cultural sensibilities and polling. The clear teachings of the Bible that the Father has presented his Son as guilt offering for our sins (Isaiah 53:10) and that the just died in the place of the unjust (1 Peter 3:18) are being mocked as a perverse idea of "cosmic child abuse."[15] Thankfully those who are faithful to Scripture are stepping up and writing helpful books and articles in response to these attacks.[16]

STANDING FIRM

In these brief pages, I hope you caught a glimpse that the reality of God's judgment of human sin for those who reject the only available payment for sin is biblical, rational, and theologically unavoidable. Next, in our continuing look at the doctrine of hell, we will need to take a sober look at what God's written revelation has told us about the nature of this punishment. Our unpleasant but necessary study of this dark side of the afterlife will continue. But for now, let us at least affirm that any temptation to sweep this truth under the carpet, to ignore it, or to brazenly choose to join the demonstration campaigning against it is futile.

God has spoken on this matter, and we must be prepared to

stand in a shrinking minority if need be. There are times in our study of God's truth when we will mourn and even cry over the proclaimed reality. We would do well to ponder with Rodin's *Poet* and soberly consider what is at stake in the urgent message of the gospel of Christ. We must be loving messengers of that gospel, compassionately speaking the truth, warning the lost in love that sin and impenitence will have consequences. Dr. Mohler's words could not be more timely for our generation as we wrestle afresh with the biblical data in a culture that rejects it:

> The temptation to revise the doctrine of hell—to remove the sting and scandal of everlasting conscious punishment—is understandable. But it is also a major test of evangelical conviction. This is no theological trifle. As one observer has asked, "Could it be that the only result of attempts, however well-meaning, to air-condition Hell, is to ensure that more and more people wind up there?" Hell demands our attention in the present, and now confronts evangelicals with a critical test of theological and biblical integrity. Hell may be denied, but it will not disappear.[17]

CHAPTER 8

Hell's Going to Be One Big Party with My Friends

Mark Twain was an example of those who would say they would prefer to go to some lush tropical island rather than to the future kingdom that God is preparing. More than that, he spoke for those we so often hear telling us that they anticipate a much better experience in hell than they would ever have in heaven. After all, they think, heaven will be filled with all those annoying Christians. As Twain put it, "heaven for climate, and hell for society."[1] As they envision it, all the fun people will be in hell, and all the guilty pleasures will be outlawed in heaven.[2]

In the seventies, Billy Joel summed up this popular perspective when he got a generation to sing along to the claim that saints are a drag and sinners are obviously more fun. Things haven't changed. Catchy bluegrass tunes from modern musicians carry titles like "In Hell I'll be in Good Company." Or go back in your mind to AC/DC's old rock anthem "Highway to Hell," or even the placards I've seen at rallies that boast, "Going to Hell and Proud." And there's also the frequently shared online graphic filled with faces of beautiful movie stars, famous atheist intellectuals, pop musicians, and a variety of anti-Christian authors accompanied by the caption: "Fear not hell, for if it exists, you'll find yourself in good company." Not only do many in our culture hold to the prevalent conception that heaven will be a dreadfully boring place, but they also think that with all the others who share their rejection of Christ they will make do in hell, and have a like-minded fellowship of cohorts with which to experience it.

This sentiment was boldly expressed in the words of the then soon-to-be executed Oklahoma City bomber Timothy McVeigh, who, as he was contemplating his fast-approaching afterlife, said in an interview that though he didn't think there was a hell, he asserted that if there was, "then I'll adapt, improvise and overcome," adding the familiar line: "I'll be in good company."[3]

With all this bluster from people who reject Christ, let us with heaviness in our hearts take a biblical look at the reality of what God said about the place commonly known as hell.

ITS NAME

The name given to the final abode of the unrepentant is "the lake of fire." This title is used six times in the book of Revelation. Other words used to describe this reality are *hell*, *the abyss*, *tartarus*, and *sheol*. All these terms are employed to refer to the place of God's judgment in the afterlife. Revelation's final descriptive title, "the lake of fire," puts the emphasis on the painful aspect Jesus spoke of in his teaching. He taught that sinners are "liable to the hell of fire" (Matthew 5:22). And he said we should seek to avoid going to "the unquenchable fire" (Mark 9:43).

One of the Greek terms used to describe this place was historically associated with fire. The word *gehenna*, used 12 times in the New Testament, calls the ancients' minds to the Valley of Hinnom adjacent to the walls of Jerusalem. There, at the worst points in Israel's history, children were sacrificed to false gods (2 Kings 23:10 and Jeremiah 7:31-32).[4] It was also the city's trash dump, and the place where residents burned animal carcasses. The sights and smells associated with this location would be the worst the inhabitants of this biblical community would have known.

The lake of fire is associated with all the unpleasant and painful realties of fire, death, stench, and loss that harken back to that awful valley. Four times the Bible uses the word "sulfur" (or brimstone) to represent its smell (Revelation 14:10; 19:20; 20:10; 21:8). The fire that represents this place is also a frequent biblical image of God's just anger toward sin. The Bible speaks of God's "burning anger" toward unrighteousness (Zephaniah 3:8). We are told of the "heat of his anger" and of judgments that are "poured out like fire" (Nahum 1:6).[5] This burning descriptive is not for the moment, but the Lord says of those who have rebelled that "their worm shall not die, their fire shall not be quenched" (Isaiah 66:24).

This lake of fiery judgment is so named to motivate us to recognize that there is nothing that can be done to adapt, improvise, or overcome the terrible nature of its reality.

LONELINESS

For all the talk of good company and partying with friends in hell, perhaps the most surprising report of this coming judgment for moderns is its loneliness. Three times in the Gospel of Matthew Jesus described hell as "outer darkness" (8:12; 22:13 and 25:30). There will be no lights, no lamps, no flashlights to even dimly illuminate a gathering.

Whatever the confines of this lake of judgment, the parameter must be of such a size that everyone faces the consequences of their own sins in isolation by themselves. Just as Christ suffered the wrath of God for our sins alone, with the sense of isolation from God and his disciples, each person will have to face their sentence in not only what is said to be darkness, but "outer darkness."

The rich man of whom Jesus spoke in Luke 16 had begun his

sentence of judgment in fixed segregation (verse 26), by himself and alone. He doesn't have company, nor does he want it. When his brothers come to mind, he doesn't wish for them to hurry to join him in an afterlife party. Rather, he begs for someone to be sent to "warn them, lest they also come into this place of torment" (verse 28).[6] The response to this request is a reminder of how many warnings already exist for his brothers, and the rest of us, in the pages of Scripture: "They have Moses and the Prophets; let them hear them" (verse 29).

All the loneliness and isolation Christians may feel in a world that rejects, maligns, and persecutes them (1 Kings 19:10; Luke 6:22; 2 Timothy 4:16) will be nothing compared to the solitary darkness that will endure for the lost. The next time you feel alone or deserted, I would encourage you to pray for those you know who need the gospel. Our dark and painful days of loneliness are periodic and are soon to be a distant memory; theirs will be ongoing and profound.

ABANDONMENT

Being separated from friends and family will be terrible, and yet it will be a relatively small concern for those in the lake of fire. The true sense of abandonment will come from the absence of God's glory.

It is true that non-Christians rarely make the connection between God and his good gifts, but as the Bible says, "Every good gift and every perfect gift is from above, coming down from the Father" (James 1:17). Every beautiful sunset, every sense of gratification from a job well done, every pleasant walk through a park, every feeling of satisfaction after a good meal, every experience of happiness and contentment is a gift from God. This is the Lord's common grace. It is a kind and unearned present from his merciful generosity. Jesus taught that God's warm sunshine is cast on both the wicked and the righteous, and his rain clouds are sent to nourish the crops of the penitent farmers as well as the obstinate ones (Matthew 5:45).

One day those good gifts will be taken away because the giver of those gifts will withdraw. This is part of the just and equitable punishment for sins. It is described as a kind of suffering that happens "away from the presence of the Lord and from the glory of his might" (2 Thessalonians 1:9). While there is an active aspect to God's righteous judgment, which I will address in a moment, this withdrawal is the passive aspect of God's judgment. Simply put, people who have lived wanting to be free from God (Psalm 2:3) will in fact be freed from God. The massive problem for them is that God is the source of all good things.

Many people now live on God's planet, breathe his air, eat the produce of his earth, and enjoy the benefits of his wisdom in a million aspects of life that they treasure—all the while rejecting him and his gift of forgiveness. One day the common grace of this life will run out. God will shut them out from his presence—the full reality of which they did not want—*and* from "the glory of his might." The "glory" of God's power and might are all around us. His power provides all good things. He sustains the systems of this world and the function of all the things we enjoy. But that day God will "step back," so to speak, and give them what they have been asking for, along with all the associated ramifications they had failed to consider.

This is the folly of those who reject God: They have each been made in God's image, their bodies have been crafted by his wisdom and design, God himself has sovereignly assigned a time and place and boundary for their habitation, in God they daily live and move and have their being—and yet they say they neither want nor need him (Acts 17:26-28). Sadly, but justly, at last they will be freed from God—freed from his power and gifts. In a word: abandoned.

RETRIBUTION

To be forsaken in the next life by the God they have discarded in this life may seem to be a just and equitable sentence, but something would be lacking in God's justice if that's all there is to the reality of hell. Beyond the passive aspect of God's judgment is something quite active. This active judgment does more than simply sequester moral criminals. God's perfect justice requires a payment. We will take a closer look at this in the next chapter, but for now, let us simply understand that the active aspect of God's "repayment" for sins is completely equitable and measured. This justice will be given, as Revelation 20:13 puts it, "according to what they had done."

UNPLEASANT

It should go without saying that everything ever revealed in Scripture about hell is miserable, painful, and unpleasant. And because Jesus gave us such vivid and identifiable portrayals of this final place of judgment, we should take a moment to let them impress our minds. For example, he repeatedly stated that "in that place there will be weeping and gnashing of teeth" (Matthew 13:50). This is a phrase the Gospel of Matthew records Jesus saying six times!

Weeping, of course, is an individual's expression of great sorrow. The same word is used of the parents who were weeping over the execution of their babies by Herod in Bethlehem (Matthew 2:18). It captures a sense of loss that cannot be consoled or comforted. It is a word used of the weeping and pain of separation (Acts 20:37). Crying of this kind causes tears of not having what one wants— it speaks of the pain of intense loss. Contrary to laughing at the obscene jokes and boisterous parties so many expect to encounter in hell, the reality is, according to Jesus, hell consists of sobbing, grieving, and heart-wrenching tears.

The expression "gnashing of teeth" has led some to think that the occupants of hell will be angry. Though this same Greek word is used one time in the New Testament to speak of people who were enraged (Acts 7:54), the frequent usage in connection with weeping leads us to believe that this is a grinding of one's teeth in pain, not anger.[7] The reaction of the lost to receiving the just penalty of their sins is not angry crying, but tears that express great loss and pain.

I can't help but think of the six references that Christ makes to hell's reality when I have that rare and unpleasant experience of being sick with the flu. The excruciating sensation of lying in bed with a fever, nausea, sore throat, and awful body aches is the one situation in which I find myself literally grinding my teeth in discomfort. Most everyone has experienced, at some point or other in their life, a kind of agony that prompts them to gnash their teeth. Jesus certainly chose to communicate the terrible experience of sin's consequences in vivid terms.

While we have not been told all the circumstances related to what a day in the lake of fire is like, we can be sure from Christ's preaching that it is exceptionally unpleasant. It should drive each of us to diligently seek the divinely provided solution for our dreadful problem with sin. It should lead God's forgiven children to be profoundly thankful for the saving confidence we have in the risen Christ.

PHYSICAL

In the same way that we tend to wrongly envision our experience in the next life as living in see-through bodies floating around on cotton-ball clouds, we often imagine hell as a place that is less concrete and tangible than the Bible says it will be. We need to remember that the resurrection of the body, the remanufacturing of the physical part of our humanity, is on the schedule for both Christians and non-Christians alike. The Bible teaches that "there will be a resurrection of both the just and the unjust" (Acts 24:15). Jesus said:

> An hour is coming when all who are in the tombs will hear his voice and come out, those who have done good to the resurrection of life, and those who have done evil to the resurrection of judgment (John 5:28-29).

It is understandable that we Christians talk so often of our forth-coming resurrection, but we should not forget that there is a pending resurrection for non-Christians as well. Recall our discussion in chapter 2 regarding God's design for our humanity. All human beings were designed to exist as body *and* spirit. The intermediate state, you'll remember, was described as a temporary period of "nakedness," so to speak. All persons will experience the untangling of body and spirit upon their physical death—but remember, this state exists only for a limited period of time.

Non-Christians will receive remanufactured bodies as well. These bodies will be impervious to physical aging or biological death. We value this as a great asset, enabling us to enjoy the pleasures and graces of the new earth in an unending way. But what is a benefit for us will be a liability for the lost. The sentient experiences of eating, drinking, walking, and embracing are all aspects of the physical nature of the New Jerusalem that we anticipate, but sadly the physical, perceptible, and tactile capacities we will enjoy will be the means of much grief for those who have rejected the gospel.

When Jesus spoke of the alarm we should rightly possess concerning hell, he said this about his Father: "Fear him who can destroy both soul and body in hell" (Matthew 10:28). The passive and active forms of God's judgment will be incurred and felt both in one's soul and body.

This compels us to conclude that hell is a physical place. The images of fire, a lake, the Valley of Hinnom, the pit, and an abyss are all meant to give us a sense of what this very real and physical place will be like. The isolation of darkness, the pain of fire, the confines of a lake, the smells of a historic valley outside of Jerusalem, the snare of a pit, and the hazards of a chasm are all ways to communicate the experience that will be had there. These biblical words should not necessarily guide our imagination to picturing its structure and its particular features. We cannot look to a forthright list of its physical dimensions, location, or material components. But because those enmeshed in physical bodies will experience physical sensations in hell, we know that the place itself will be physical too.

CONSCIOUS

One of the most detailed stories recorded in the Gospels is a story that Jesus told about the conscious experience that two men had in the afterlife. The account of the rich man and Lazarus tells of the conscious comfort and the conscious suffering that commences in the intermediate state, prior to the resurrection of the body and the specific judgment of each life—topics we will look at in the next chapter.

Jesus begins his teaching with these words:

> There was a rich man who was clothed in purple and fine linen and who feasted sumptuously every day. And at his gate was laid a poor man named Lazarus, covered with sores, who desired to be fed with what fell from the rich man's table. Moreover, even the dogs came and licked his sores. The poor man died and was carried by the angels to Abraham's side. The rich man also died and was buried, and in Hades, being in torment, he lifted up his eyes and saw Abraham far off and Lazarus at his side. And he called out, "Father Abraham, have mercy on me, and send Lazarus to dip the end of his finger in water and cool my tongue, for I am in anguish in this flame." But Abraham said, "Child, remember that you in your lifetime received your good things, and Lazarus in like manner bad things; but now he is comforted here, and you are in anguish" (Luke 16:19-25).

There is no soul sleep for the saved, and no annihilation of the lost. The scenario authoritatively given by Christ here is one of people being ushered into one of two places—one characterized by relief and consolation (called Abraham's side), and the other of anguish and distress (called Hades). These two places were habitations during the intermediate state of Christ's day. Abraham's words to the rich man show us something of the extent of his consciousness. Not only does he know where he is and later expresses his concern that his brothers don't arrive there, but he is also said to have memories of his earthly life. He is asked by Abraham to recall his life of luxury, and later in the account we see that he is well aware of the fact that he has five yet-to-die brothers.

This conscious existence doesn't diminish the forthcoming resurrection of his body; instead, it could be argued that it is heightened. Faculties of thoughts, feelings, memories, and concerns are all attributed to this man who rejected the truth of God's Word in his former life.

ETERNAL AND PERMANENT

The detailed story that Christ tells of the afterlife continues:

> "And besides all this, between us and you a great chasm has been fixed, in order that those who would pass from here to you may not be able, and none may cross from there to us." And he said, "Then I beg you, father, to send him to my father's house—for I have five brothers—so that he may warn them, lest they also come into this place of torment" (verses 26-28).

The fixed nature of this place of judgment is stressed by Christ. Throughout Scripture there is an emphasis on the urgency of grappling with the call of the gospel in *this* life. "Today, if you hear his voice, do not harden your hearts as in the rebellion, on the day of testing in the wilderness" (Hebrews 3:7-8). As the book of Hebrews warns, "It is appointed for man to die once, and after that comes judgment" (9:27).

The urgent call of responding obediently to the gospel is under-scored by the permanence and eternality of the two destinations. Notice the parity and correspondence drawn between the two all the way back to the Old Testament: "Many of those who sleep in the dust of the earth shall awake, some to everlasting life, and some to shame and everlasting contempt" (Daniel 12:2). The duration of this kind of "life" is throughout the Bible equated to the experi-ence of those resurrected to the existence of shame and everlasting contempt.

Don't be tempted to dismiss the eternal and permanent nature of the conscious and resurrected existence of the lost, simply because the word "life" is also enlisted to describe our lives in the New Jeru-salem. Both death and life are designations of a kind of life. Ephe-sians 2 speaks of a kind of life here and now that is "dead" to God (verse 1). The paths of life and death have always been laid before us as two ways to consciously proceed: "I have set before you today life and good, death and evil" (Deuteronomy 30:15). Just as Jesus spoke of "storing up treasure in heaven," elsewhere the Bible describes liv-ing in that place of enjoying the dividends as "that which is truly life" (1 Timothy 6:18-19). Even now, Jesus calls the biologically liv-ing to step out of the domain of "death" and into the arena of "life": "Truly, truly, I say to you, whoever hears my word and believes him who sent me has eternal life. He does not come into judgment, but has passed from death to life" (John 5:24).

The lost will be consigned permanently, physically, and con-sciously to experience a kind of *living* that is described as death. Revelation 20:14 states it succinctly: "This is the second death, the lake of fire." The parting of these two eternal destinies are mirrored in their permanence and duration. Jesus spoke to this when he described the entrance of the saved into their final home: "Then the King will say to those on his right, 'Come, you who are blessed by my Father, inherit the kingdom prepared for you from the foun-dation of the world'" (Matthew 25:34). Later in that teaching he turned to those on his left and said, "Depart from me, you cursed, into the eternal fire prepared for the devil and his angels" (verse 41). The correspondence of these two is summed up with his concluding statement: "And these will go away into eternal punishment, but the righteous into eternal life" (verse 46). The duration of the punishment is the same as the duration of the experience in God's kingdom—eternal.

When we speak of eternity, we might wrongly think that there will be no sense of time marching on. That is not how the afterlife is presented in the Bible—neither in reference to heaven nor to hell. The following passage describes what will take place before the 1,000-year reign of Christ we considered in the previous chapter. It speaks of the political and religious world leaders receiving their place of punishment:

> The beast was captured, and with it the false prophet who in its presence had done the signs by which he deceived those who had received the mark of the beast and those who worshiped its image. These two were thrown alive into the lake of fire that burns with sulfur (Revelation 19:20).

Notice that *after* 1,000 years, Satan himself will be permanently delivered to that same place.

> The devil who had deceived them was thrown into the lake of fire and sulfur where the beast and the false prophet were, and they will be tormented day and night forever and ever (Revelation 20:10).

The political and religious leaders are still there 1,000 years later, and in case there was any confusion about the ongoing nature of this place of judgment, Scripture adds to the description that the torment which provokes weeping and gnashing of teeth will continue "day and night forever and ever." This indicates that in eternity, we will sense the continuation of time.

> *Our study of the nature of God's coming judgment can and should arouse us to take the good news to those next door and around the world.*

THE CHRISTIAN RESPONSE

Moving from Hades or the lake of fire to the New Jerusalem is impossible. This again should heighten our interest in the vital work of evangelism. Unfortunately, our spiritual predecessors of decades and centuries past had an evangelistic and missionary zeal that the modern church seems to lack today. If only we could catch a glimpse of what God so diligently presents to us in the pages of his Word—namely, that there are only two destinations, they are very real, and they are both very permanent. Perhaps a more immediate awareness of these sobering truths would reignite our generation to proclaim the good news with passion, sincerity, and consistency. God has provided an eternal solution to an eternal problem. Our study of the nature of God's coming judgment can and should arouse us to take the good news to those next door and around the world.

Allow me to end this brief survey of God's forthcoming response to the unrepentant with a couple excerpts from a sermon you may have heard about, but few have taken the time to read. It was delivered in Connecticut, on July 8, 1741. It was a message based on the pastor's study of the realities of hell. It was hard-hitting and urgent, springing from a heart of compassion for the lost. In light of the biblical truths we have just reviewed, take these words in the spirit in which they were originally given.

Perhaps reading this excerpt in light of the passages of Scripture we have been studying will embolden you to strongly object to our culture's characterization of this 275-year-old sermon as an angry rant from an uptight preacher, nursing a distorted view of God. This is what Jonathan Edwards stated in his sermon entitled, "Sinners in the Hands of an Angry God."

> The use of this awful subject may be for awakening unconverted persons in this congregation. This that you have heard is the case of every one of you that are out of Christ. —That world of misery, that lake of burning brimstone, is extended abroad under you. There is the dreadful pit of the glowing flames of the wrath of God; there is hell's wide gaping mouth open; and you have nothing to stand upon, nor any thing to take hold of; there is nothing between you and hell but the air; it is only the power and mere pleasure of God that holds you up.

> You probably are not sensible of this; you find you are kept out of hell, but do not see the hand of God in it; but look at other things, as the good state of your bodily constitution, your care of your own life, and the means you use for your own preservation. But indeed these things are nothing; if God should withdraw his hand, they would avail no more to keep you from falling, than the thin air to hold up a person that is suspended in it.

> Your wickedness makes you as it were heavy as lead, and to tend downwards with great weight and pressure towards hell; and if God should let you go, you would immediately sink and swiftly descend and plunge into the bottomless gulf; and your healthy constitution, and your own care and prudence, and best contrivance, and all your righteousness, would have no more influence to uphold you and keep you out of hell, than a spider's

web would have to stop a falling rock. Were it not for
the sovereign pleasure of God, the earth would not bear
you one moment; for you are a burden to it: the creation groans with you; the creature is made subject to
the bondage of your corruption, not willingly; the sun
does not willingly shine upon you to give you light to
serve sin and Satan; the earth does not willingly yield her
increase to satisfy your lusts; nor is it willingly a stage for
your wickedness to be acted upon; the air does not willingly serve you for breath to maintain the flame of life
in your vitals, while you spend your life in the service of
God's enemies. God's creatures are good, and were made
for men to serve God with, and do not willingly subserve
to any other purpose, and groan when they are abused
to purposes so directly contrary to their nature and end.
And the world would spew you out, were it not for the
sovereign hand of him who hath subjected it in hope.
There are the black clouds of God's wrath now hanging directly over your heads, full of the dreadful storm,
and big with thunder; and were it not for the restrain-
ing hand of God, it would immediately burst forth upon
you. The sovereign pleasure of God, for the present, stays
his rough wind; otherwise it would come with fury, and
your destruction would come like a whirlwind, and you
would be like the chaff of the summer threshing-floor...

And now you have an extraordinary opportunity, a day
wherein Christ has thrown the door of mercy wide open,
and stands in calling, and crying with a loud voice to
poor sinners; a day wherein many are flocking to him,
and pressing into the kingdom of God. Many are daily
coming from the east, west, north, and south; many that
were very lately in the same miserable condition that you
are in, are now in a happy state, with their hearts filled

with love to him who has loved them, and washed them from their sins in his own blood, and rejoicing in hope of the glory of God. How awful it is to be left behind at such a day! To see so many others feasting, while you are pining and perishing! To see so many rejoicing and singing for joy of heart, while you have cause to mourn for sorrow of heart, and howl for vexation of spirit! How can you rest one moment in such a condition?...

Therefore, let every one that is out of Christ, now awake and fly from the wrath to come. The wrath of Almighty God is now undoubtedly hanging over a great part of this congregation. Let every one fly out of Sodom: "Haste and escape for your lives, look not behind you, escape to the mountain, lest you be consumed."[8]

CHAPTER 9

Hell Is the Exact Same Terrible Experience for Everyone

H ell, no doubt, is a terrible experience, as we have been working to understand. But a careful consideration of what the Bible says will help us to see that God's justice and equity will not allow hell to be the exact same experience for everyone who goes there. To better grasp how God's justice will be carried out, we need to make sure we are clear about who is *not* in charge in this place called hell.

SATAN IS NOT IN CHARGE

Most caricatures of hell show the confined occupants of this fiery underworld as suffering under the cloven hoof of Satan. With horned head and red cape, he clenches his pitchfork as he barks commands at all his doomed subjects. So goes the prevalent conception in cartoons, movies, and maybe even your own mind. But that's not what the Bible says.

In the current age, Satan does have tremendous power. For now he is called the "god of this world" (2 Corinthians 4:4). Presently he is labeled as "the prince of the power of the air" and "the spirit that is now at work in the sons of disobedience" (Ephesians 2:2). We are assured that we are God's and "from God," but as for the rest of the world, it "lies in the power of the evil one" (1 John 5:19). Perhaps it is all these biblical depictions of Satan's present-day reign that keeps us from recognizing how powerless he will soon be.

The life, death, and resurrection of Christ sealed Satan's fate. The game has already been won, but the clock is still running. Satan continues his "reign" on the playing field of earth like a madman until his time is up. The book of Revelation speaks of the day when "the kingdom of the world has become the kingdom of our Lord and of his Christ, and he shall reign forever and ever" (Revelation 11:15). Then the devil's earthly power will come to an end. And the adversary's leadership over God's creation is forever halted.

Here's how heaven will respond:

> The twenty-four elders who sit on their thrones before God fell on their faces and worshiped God, saying, "We give thanks to you, Lord God Almighty, who is and who was, for you have taken your great power and begun to reign. The nations raged, but your wrath came, and the time for the dead to be judged, and for rewarding your servants, the prophets and saints, and those who fear your name, both small and great, and for destroying the destroyers of the earth" (verses 16-18).

Satan and his henchmen have been tempting, persuading, lying, and effecting death and destruction on the inhabitants of the earth beginning from the third chapter of the Bible. And at this future point on God's prophetic calendar, it will all come to an end. Satan will be judged, along with his demonic band, and all will be consigned to their own judgment in the lake of fire. The promise of God is that one day "the devil who had deceived them [will be] thrown into the lake of fire and sulfur where the beast and the false prophet [are], and they will be tormented day and night forever and ever" (Revelation 20:10). The devil will be cast into this place of God's judgment not to rule over it, but to be a subject of it.

> *Everything that takes place in hell will be measured by God's justice, not Satan's decisions.*

To incur the just retribution of God—that is why hell was created in the first place. It is not a place for anyone to exercise leadership or to rule over others. People are relocated to this final abode for the same reason as Satan and his demons—as a place of just, equitable, and fair repayment for sins. When Jesus spoke of people entering hell's punishment, he reminded us of its initial purpose: "Then he will say to those on his left, 'Depart from me, you cursed, into the eternal fire prepared for the devil and his angels'" (Matthew 25:41).

So then, hell is not a place where lost people are turned over to the maniacal domain of Satan. He will not be in charge. Everything that takes place there will be measured by God's justice, not Satan's decisions. Daily life in the lake of fire will not be under the jurisdiction of the devil. He will have zero autonomy or authority, just like every other lonely inhabitant of that place.

CRIMES AND PUNISHMENTS

To get a sense of the experience for the unrepentant in the afterlife, we must reconsider the laws and penalties that are articulated at various places in the Bible.

When the Israelites were freed from Egypt in the fifteenth century before Christ, they were called out by God to become their own nation. They were a huge group of people, and God promised to take them to their own spacious land. But what they didn't have was a civil law code. To function as a just and equitable society, they needed a codified set of ethical rules and just penalties, a definition of a set of prosecutable crimes and their corresponding punishments.

Along with these civil laws the people of Israel were also given a list of ceremonial laws—rules that many people like to talk about and criticize. These were to symbolically represent their religious identification and mark them as distinct from other nations. These ceremonial laws included such things as dietary restrictions, rules for haircuts, animal sacrifices, required fringes on their clothes, along with other specific regulations, and were all practices designed to symbolize the truths regarding their coming redemption and their spiritual devotion to God.

All the ceremonial laws culminated in Christ and came to an end in the first century AD. They were said to be "a shadow of the good things to come instead of the true form of these realities" (Hebrews 10:1). So all the festivals, diets, symbols, and special days have been supplanted by Jesus Christ and our trust in him, and they are no longer binding for those who look to the Bible as their authority (Colossians 2:16-17).

At many points within the civil and ceremonial laws we can see the reflection of God's good and righteous character. Therefore, we can glean a third set of principles and precepts as we read these Old Testament civil and ceremonial laws—as well as some direct exhortations that stand on their own as moral directives. It is not hard to see that many of the Old Testament civil laws were based on moral expectations and assumptions. For instance, a person was required to return a fellow Israelite's cloak to him by sunset, even if it was taken as a pledge in a financial transaction, because it "is his only covering, and it is his cloak for his body; in what else shall he sleep? And if he cries to me, I will hear, for I am compassionate" (Exodus 22:26-27). Compassionate and sympathetic concern for your neighbor is a moral directive throughout the Bible, but here it is reflected in the nation's code related to money lending.

Remembering that the specific civil code we see in the Old Testament was given to a people who were to function as a nation among other nations is very important. The New Testament church, on the other hand, was founded by Christ as an international organization with active participants from all the nations around the world. As Christians from various nations, we have been called to submit to the civil laws of our own respective countries (unless, of course, those laws obligate us to disobey God—Acts 5:27-29). By God's common grace, often most of a nation's civil laws reflect the moral virtues that correspond with the law of God etched on the human conscience (Romans 2:14-15).

For that reason, we can rightly be instructed to submit to the governing authorities, knowing that

> rulers are not a terror to good conduct, but to bad. Would you have no fear of the one who is in authority? Then do what is good, and you will receive his approval, for he is God's servant for your good. But if you do wrong, be afraid, for he does not bear the sword in vain. For he is the servant of God, an avenger who carries out God's wrath on the wrongdoer. Therefore one must be in subjection, not only to avoid God's wrath but also for the sake of conscience (Romans 13:3-5).

I give all that background to make the simple point that the civil code of the Old Testament nation of Israel, and even the criminal and penal codes of the state or country we live in, can help to inform us of the nature of God's implementation of earthly *moral* crimes and the punishments they have earned in the afterlife. Consider, for instance, Israel's Old Testament law that required a full one-to-one restitution if someone's animal was negligently let loose from its pen and grazed in a neighbor's field (Exodus 22:5). If, however, the problem arose on account of theft, a shady business deal, or someone was ripped off by being lied to, or through some other false means, the penalty was full restitution *plus* 20 percent (Leviticus 6:1-5). These kinds of distinctions are common in the Old Testament.

For example, if you were responsible for the death of another human being, you might be charged with manslaughter, which was punishable by imprisonment in what was called a "city of refuge" (see Deuteronomy 19:1-7). But if you committed premeditated murder with hatred in your heart, the law declared that you had to pay with your own life (Numbers 35:20-21). Thus motives were taken into account. Negligence was also taken into account. If you tolerated unnecessary hazards that caused another's injury (Deuteronomy 22:8), or if you had previous warning of a liability, such as the aggressive and harmful pattern of an animal you owned (Exodus 21:29), the penalty would be greater.

These are just few examples of the varied consequences for different kinds of transgressions due to varying circumstances. We could spend a lot of time observing the principle of varied penalties and punishments by going online and viewing the rules and retributions of apartment complexes, homeowners' associations, municipal codes, state penal codes, or the federal sentencing guidelines of our country.

Human authorities, judges, and juries are to do their best at ascertaining liabilities and motives, as well as the mitigating and special circumstances relating to all the crimes that may concern lying, cheating, stealing, and killing. They are then to try to mete out the appropriate penalties, sanctions, fines, and punishments. Humans do this imperfectly. God will do this perfectly, at an event called the Great White Throne Judgment.

ISN'T ALL SIN EQUALLY SINFUL?

If you grew up like I did with a lot of sound-bite theology from Sunday school, all this discussion about the differences that exist between sins and the magnitude of their punishments might be surprising. You may have heard that in God's eyes, all sins are equally sinful. After all, doesn't God look at all sinners with equal disdain because he is a perfectly holy God who cannot tolerate any sin whatsoever?

If that's true, then you would be right to think that hell will be the same exact terrible experience for everyone. If all varieties of sinners end up in hell because their sins were not forgiven, and all sin is viewed the same by God, then every sinner will have an identical experience. But that is not what the Bible tells us about God's final judgment of the lost.

The assumption that all sin is the same is derived from a couple of New Testament passages that speak not about God's just retribution, but about people's temptation to think that their particular sins are not bad enough to qualify them as sinners. All sin, of course, is sin. Categorically it is all unacceptable. The Christians that James was addressing in his letter were being confronted about their sin of partiality—specifically, their tendency to give special treatment, the best seats, and the warmest greetings to the rich Christians among them. God condemned this as sin, and James reminded them that any and every sin should be taken seriously. He wrote:

> If you show partiality, you are committing sin and are convicted by the law as transgressors. For whoever keeps the whole law but fails in one point has become guilty of all of it. For he who said, "Do not commit adultery," also said, "Do not murder." If you do not commit adultery but do murder, you have become a transgressor of the law (James 2:9-11).

We cannot dismiss some sins as unimportant because any sin, regardless of the severity, can put our fellowship with God out of step. That's not to say that sin does not come in varying degrees of severity; it does. And God will rightly respond with varying degrees of punishment.

In the book of Galatians, Christians were called out for a similar kind of misunderstanding. They thought that as long as they avoided the *big* violations of God's major rules, God would accept them for keeping most of them. Some among them thought that they could be considered right before God by maintaining what they considered to be the most important biblical commands. If pressed, they would have to admit they couldn't keep every last rule in the Bible. But they were hoping (like so many people today) that God would grade on a curve. This passage was penned to them:

> All who rely on works of the law are under a curse; for it is written, "Cursed be everyone who does not abide by all things written in the Book of the Law, and do them." Now it is evident that no one is justified before God by the law, for "The righteous shall live by faith" (Galatians 3:10-11).

Acceptance from a holy God requires a holy life. And even the best among us fall short. What we need is a complete replacement of our individual lives. That is what Christ came to provide—a life of perfect righteousness and holiness. Reliance on his life, trust in him, faith in his righteousness is what the Bible says is required for this great exchange. God will fully qualify us for his presence by legally replacing each of our imperfect lives with the perfect life of his Son.

Imagine it like this: You are a quality-control inspector for a windshield manufacturer. You sit at the end of the manufacturing line, looking carefully at each windshield that comes off the conveyer belt. The owner only allows unbroken windshields to be shipped from his company—obviously! You have to make sure each windshield meets the boss's standard. Because the demand is unbroken windshields, it wouldn't matter whether you saw a windshield with a small chip, a medium-sized crack, or gigantic smashed section right in the middle of it. Broken is broken!

It is the same way with sin. Sin disqualifies us before God regarding our justification, and should rightly get our attention. Any "chip," "crack," or "break" is a problem. For non-Christians, any sin should inform them that they need Christ's righteous life to replace theirs. For Christians, any sin should drive us to repentance and confession so that our daily communion with the Lord will not be impeded. But with regard to the non-Christian's judgment on the last day, or even the discipline a believer receives from God, the fact the Bible speaks of the magnitude and severity of sins cannot and should not be overlooked. If God were to make no distinctions between the various sins people commit, then there would be no need for the day of detailed individual evaluation, known in the Bible as the Great White Throne judgment.

THE GREAT WHITE THRONE

After the series of promised end-time events, and just before the unveiling of the New Jerusalem, there will come a time of judgment, which is described in this way:

> I saw a great white throne and him who was seated on it. From his presence earth and sky fled away, and no place was found for them. And I saw the dead, great and small, standing before the throne, and books were opened. Then another book was opened, which is the book of life. And the dead were judged by what was written in the books, according to what they had done. And the sea gave up the dead who were in it, Death and Hades gave up the dead who were in them, and they were judged, each one of them, according to what they had done. Then Death and Hades were thrown into the lake of fire. This is the second death, the lake of

> fire. And if anyone's name was not found written in the
> book of life, he was thrown into the lake of fire (Reve-
> lation 20:11-15).

Several books are mentioned in this passage. Let's start by notic-
ing the last one listed. This book is most critical. If your name is not
found written in "the book of life," then there is no escaping the destination we are now studying. If your name is not in that book, you
will be going to the lake of fire. But this text teaches us that one's
condition there will depend on what is written in the other books.

It is clear enough that one of the books mentioned must be a
record of each person's deeds, because the scene is presented as people being evaluated based on "what they had done" (verse 12). This
is a common theme in Scripture—the maintenance of a register
of human actions[1] (for example, Psalm 56:8; Malachi 3:16). Jesus
warned that every aspect of a lost person's life will be evaluated on
this day, even the words he or she has uttered: "I tell you, on the day
of judgment people will give account for every careless word they
speak" (Matthew 12:36).

Another book (or set of books) referred to by the plural use of
the word "books" is the record of what God has said. Jesus spoke
of a standard on judgment day: "The one who rejects me and does
not receive my words has a judge; the word that I have spoken will
judge him on the last day" (John 12:48). Christ said the same of the
words in the Old Testament: "Do not think that I will accuse you
to the Father. There is one who accuses you: Moses, on whom you
have set your hope" (John 5:45).

Certainly, God's Word is the unchanging measure by which people's thoughts, words, and actions will be evaluated. The Bible says
that even those who do not have the details of God's written Word,
in reality, live each day with a reflection of those principles, precepts,
and moral requirements imprinted on their consciences. The Bible
says the evidence of this is found in the way people internally accuse

themselves when they do wrong, or quietly justify themselves when they know they have done right. Here is how it is stated:

> When Gentiles, who do not have the law, by nature do what the law requires, they are a law to themselves, even though they do not have the law. They show that the work of the law is written on their hearts, while their conscience also bears witness, and their conflicting thoughts accuse or even excuse them on that day when, according to my gospel, God judges the secrets of men by Christ Jesus (Romans 2:14-16).

Everyone whose name is not inscribed in the book of life will have his personal book of actions assessed in light of the book of God's truth. This will determine what kind of punishment they have earned. As happens with a courtroom docket, along with a record of charges and a record of the laws that should have been kept, each person will face the Judge to be fittingly sentenced.

Scripture makes it clear that God is just and will punish people appropriately according to their violations: "Give to them according to their work and according to the evil of their deeds; give to them according to the work of their hands; render them their due reward" (Psalm 28:4). This is what Jesus promised is coming at the end of the age: "Behold, I am coming soon, bringing my recompense with me, to repay each one for what he has done" (Revelation 22:12).

MITIGATING FACTORS

As in modern courtrooms, there are many factors taken into consideration during the sentencing phase of a trial. Again, Jesus spoke specifically as to how this will work when all the lost are gathered before the Great White Throne. When he sent his 12 apostles out into the villages and towns of Israel to preach the good news of repentance and forgiveness, Jesus stated that if a town rejected their clear and urgent preaching, then "it will be more bearable on the day of judgment for the land of Sodom and Gomorrah than for that town" (Matthew 10:15).

Here the apostles were reminded of the most notoriously evil and immoral cities in the book of Genesis. If some average settlement in first-century Israel were to reject the call to repent and trust in Christ to be saved, their judgment and sentencing at the Great White Throne would be worse than it will be for the people of those wild and morally wicked ancient cities. Why? Because the first-century Israelites had explicit knowledge and an urgent call from God's ambassadors to repent, while the citizens of Sodom and Gomorrah only had the testimony of God in conscience and creation. Both groups of people will be liable on the day of judgment, but their judgment will differ based on the amount of revelation they possessed about what it means to repent and trust God for a solution.

But what if Peter, James, and John were not as clear as they should have been? What if their logic, persuasion, or passion didn't perfectly represent the call of Christ? What would it be like for that town on judgment day if the presentation of the solution to sin's problem were not as crystal clear as it should have been? A chapter later, Jesus answered that question by mentioning the cities where he himself was not only a perfect preacher, but he also provided confirmation of his deity through miracles. Jesus spoke about those places and compared them, again, to the city of Sodom, along with some of the infamous enemies that taunted and fought against Old Testament Israel.

> Then he began to denounce the cities where most of his mighty works had been done, because they did not repent. "Woe to you, Chorazin! Woe to you, Bethsaida! For if the mighty works done in you had been done in Tyre and Sidon, they would have repented long ago in sackcloth and ashes. But I tell you, it will be more

bearable on the day of judgment for Tyre and Sidon than for you. And you, Capernaum, will you be exalted to heaven? You will be brought down to Hades. For if the mighty works done in you had been done in Sodom, it would have remained until this day. But I tell you that it will be more tolerable on the day of judgment for the land of Sodom than for you" (Matthew 11:20-24).

These sorts of statements from Christ not only affirm that judgments will vary for different people, they also confirm that particular sins may be judged less strictly in one case, but more so in other cases—based on a person's knowledge and exposure to the truth. Jesus upheld this principle in a parable designed to communicate the importance of responding obediently to his instructions. In the story he spoke of a servant who "knew his master's will but did not get ready" and one who "did not know" all the clear expressions of his will. The two servants were punished differently: one receiving a "severe beating," and the other "a light beating" (Luke 12:47-48). It was in this context that Christ gave the well-remembered line: "Everyone to whom much was given, of him much will be required, and from him to whom they entrusted much, they will demand the more" (verse 48).

While that principle may be applied to different situations in life, the original context is the increased responsibility and moral culpability people have based on their exposure to the clear testimony of the truth. This point is also made in Romans 2:12: "All who have sinned without the law will also perish without the law, and all who have sinned under the law will be judged by the law." Of course, we cannot divorce this from the broader points being made in the book of Romans. People cannot say, "I should not be judged at all because I didn't know what was right and wrong."[2] The point of Romans 1 is that even the fallen created universe is an adequate testimony to beauty, order, symmetry, and righteousness so that those who can observe it all and yet still refuse to repent are "without excuse" (Romans 1:19-20; see also Psalm 19). And Romans 2 is making the point that people are endowed with a conscience that reflects God's moral standards. We are warned about what will happen when we willfully violate our conscience: "Because of your hard and impenitent heart you are storing up wrath for yourself on the day of wrath when God's righteous judgment will be revealed" (verse 5).

Now, the principles relating to the severity or moderation of punishment apply only to the lost, not to Christians. Still, the whole matter of varying degrees of punishment should have no bearing on our diligence when it comes to sharing the gospel. Romans 10 makes it clear that the gospel message *must* go forth and people must repent and trust in Christ to have their names written in the book of life. The knowledge of this end goal is what has fueled and motivated generations of Christian missions. May our clarity on this point continue to spur us on.[3]

> For "everyone who calls on the name of the Lord will be saved." How then will they call on him in whom they have not believed? And how are they to believe in him of whom they have never heard? And how are they to hear without someone preaching? And how are they to preach unless they are sent? As it is written, "How beautiful are the feet of those who preach the good news!" But they have not all obeyed the gospel. For Isaiah says, "Lord, who has believed what he has heard from us?" So faith comes from hearing, and hearing through the word of Christ (verses 13-17).

ETERNAL CONSEQUENCES?

If this is the first time you have thought through the mitigating factors that will be a part of the Great White Throne judgment, you might be tempted to think, *Maybe then it's not that bad after all.* Let me remind you that Jesus said we should *never* think that way about the judgment to come: "I will warn you whom to fear: fear him who, after he has killed, has authority to cast into hell. Yes, I tell you, fear him!" (Luke 12:5).

While God's equity and justice will always ensure that the retribution for sin is measured and appropriate, we must remember that these sins are committed against a holy, transcendent, and eternal God. And, as the Bible so clearly states, this reality is as eternal and ongoing as the experience of the saved in the New Jerusalem (Matthew 25:46). It is depicted as occurring "day and night forever and ever" (Revelation 20:10).

This one fact is the reason many people dismiss the concept of hell altogether. How can these moral crimes on earth, which take a finite amount of time to commit, earn for people an eternity of retribution? While this is a common question, and while it is the reason many dismiss the biblical teaching on the duration of hell outright, it certainly is not the way people think when they are victims of a crime. No one goes into an earthly courtroom to try to determine a punishment based on questions like, "How long did the rape take to commit?" or "How much time elapsed during the stabbing?" or "How many seconds was his fist in contact with your chin?" We don't call it equity if we penalize people based on the amount of time it took to commit the crime. As others have written with regard to the just response of God to sin: "The extent of punishment corresponds not with the time taken to commit the crime, but with the nature of the crime and the person against whom the crime was committed."[4]

Imagine receiving a call from the school your son attends, and it is reported that he was in trouble because he hit someone in the face. I assume you would brace yourself for the kind of trouble he was in. For starters, remember, it takes only a second to haul off and hit someone in the nose. But let's say your son hit someone in the face as the result of some silly dispute. You would naturally want to know all the details of what had happened. And because his action was a violation of the school rules, you are told he is being suspended for the rest of the day. So you would get in your car, go to school, and pick him up.

But suppose it wasn't a fellow student that your son slugged in the face, but one of his teachers. You would probably gasp upon receiving that news, and you would rightly brace yourself for consequences, which would be far worse than an afternoon's suspension.

Let's take this further. Suppose the person your son hit wasn't a fellow student, or even a teacher, but in fact the principal of the school. I am sure you would swallow hard and expect an even greater punishment.

Or, imagine amid your busy afternoon getting a call in which you are told your son had gotten into trouble, was sent to the principal, then the sheriff's department was called on account of the serious nature of what your son had done, and during a question-and-answer session with the deputy, your son hauled off and slugged the deputy in the face! You would be in a very different frame of mind about what might come next.

Consider yet another scenario: Imagine your son commits an offense, is told to report to the principal, and the police are called in. They in turn haul your son to juvenile hall, and your son slugs the county judge in the face.

Do you see what's happening here?

As Jonathan Edwards rightly pointed out in his much-maligned sermon of 1741, "the greatest earthly potentates, in their greatest majesty and strength, and when clothed in their greatest terrors, are but feeble, despicable worms of the dust, in comparison of the great and almighty Creator and King of heaven and earth."[5] Ultimately, the sins we commit are done against the clear directives of the King of the Universe. As David said in his contrition, "Against you, you only, have I sinned and done what is evil in your sight, so that you may be justified in your words and blameless in your judgment" (Psalm 51:4).[6]

AN APPROPRIATE REALITY

Today's prisons are filled with people who believe their sentences are unjust. Having preached to incarcerated inmates throughout my years of ministry, I find it is not the norm to have tried, convicted, and sentenced criminals tell you that their situation is as it ought to be. But I know from heaven's perspective (and I suspect even from hell's viewpoint) there will be a sense of perfect propriety about the realities of hell. I am not saying it is not a sad reality, but I believe that after each individual personally encounters God, either as gracious Savior or as holy Judge, there will be clarity about the equitable and suitable arrangement in eternity.

Even during the worst of the unfolding of God's earthly judgments—according to Revelation 16:5-6—we read of the holy angels mediating these awful judgments with these words:

> Just are you, O Holy One, who is and who was, for you brought these judgments. For they have shed the blood of saints and prophets, and you have given them blood to drink. It is what they deserve!

Prior to that encounter with God, the people sensing the just judgments of the Lord are found blaming him and cursing his name (verses 8-11). But I am fairly confident there will be no fists shaken at God after the perfectly just trial and sentencing of each individual life. They will most likely realize, as the angels in Revelation 16 say, that this is indeed what is deserved.

For us, there will be no doubt. The eternal recognition of grace that the Bible says we will all sense and express is a guarantee in itself that we will have the perspective of Revelation 16. We will know that we have violated the holiness of the Creator and Ruler of all things, and that we rightly deserve punishment as well (Ephesians 1:3-14). Yet knowing what we deserve, we will praise him for his amazing grace.

Amazing grace! how sweet the sound,
   That saved a wretch like me!
I once was lost, but now am found,
   Was blind, but now I see.
'Twas grace that taught my heart to fear,
   And grace my fears relieved;
How precious did that grace appear
   The hour I first believed![7]

CHAPTER 10

It Doesn't Matter What Happens to My Body After I Die

When I was a child, during our annual cross-country family vacation I was dragged along to the old country church my cousins and great-uncle and aunt attended in the deep South. Growing up in the suburbs of Southern California, I wasn't used to walking past headstones of the dead as I arrived at church. One summer, after the morning sermon, my mother took me on a tour of all the burial plots of our relatives' bodies in the churchyard. While it was interesting to hear stories about them, still I thought it was rather odd that every weekend, the people who attended that church would be reminded of their loved ones' deaths as they walked from and to the parking lot.

Since becoming a pastor, my perspective has changed. Given that our church is in suburban Southern California, I am sure we will never be granted a permit to start our own graveyard adjacent to the church auditorium. But at least now I understand the value of what my spiritual forefathers used to do. Churchyards were nothing new to the American South. And for centuries all over the world,

Christian churches that were fortunate enough to acquire property and build buildings usually included an associated graveyard—it was a reflection of their theology, their eschatology in particular, and their Christian worldview in general. Church, after all, was ultimately about eternal matters, subjects of supreme importance, and weighty concerns related to heaven and hell.

When we go to church, we are to be reminded of the exhortation to "seek the things that are above, where Christ is, seated at the right hand of God" (Colossians 3:1). We should be hearing sermons that say, "Set your minds on things that are above, not on things that are on earth. For you have died, and your life is hidden with Christ in God. When Christ who is your life appears, then you also will appear with him in glory" (verses 2-4). Our time in worship and in the Scriptures should remind us that by faith we have been united to Christ's death and "we shall certainly be united with him in a resurrection like his" (Romans 6:5). We should be motivated to be "eagerly waiting" for his second coming (Hebrews 9:28), which should bolster our confidence that

> we who are alive, who are left until the coming of the Lord, will not precede those who have fallen asleep. For the Lord himself will descend from heaven with a cry of command, with the voice of an archangel, and with the sound of the trumpet of God. And the dead in Christ will rise first. Then we who are alive, who are left, will be caught up together with them in the clouds to meet the Lord in the air, and so we will always be with the Lord (1 Thessalonians 4:15-17).

It makes much more sense to me now, as a Bible teacher trying to keep the church from devolving into a self-help convention, that somewhere between finding a parking spot and receiving that first Sunday morning handshake, we would do well to have a palpable reminder of what our theology is really all about.

You may say, "In a matter of months, those headstones would become an invisible part of the church landscape." I don't think so. Just today I reached out to two people in my congregation who had lost family members on this very date two years ago. Like most pastors, I try to track these important days of loss on my calendar. Not a single time have I called, emailed, or texted (even four, five, and six years down the road) and had my congregant say, "I'd forgotten today was the day." No, people remember the death of their loved ones. And how striking it would be for us to be reminded of these foundational matters as we gather to worship and learn of our Creator.

I am *not* saying that a church without a cemetery should include one in their next master plan. That season of architectural design is long gone. But I *am* saying that our understanding of death, the ceremonies related to the passing of our loved ones, and what we as a culture do with their deceased bodies says something important about our faith, our theology, and our values.

CREMATION

The burning of deceased human bodies has a long history. It has been an enduring feature of the ancient religion of Hinduism. The Hindu practice is called *Antyesti*, which literally means "the last sacrifice." It is performed with its associated rituals, preferably within 24 hours of death. Hindus believe in reincarnation and teach that the fire and accompanying religious rites sever one's ties to earthly life and give momentum to the soul for its continuing spiritual journey.[1] The early Vedic period of Hinduism was known to be a fire cult which believed that purity emerges from fire, and this is said to have had an influence on the Hindu practice of cremation of the dead.[2]

In cultures impacted by Judaism, Christianity, and Islam, burial of the dead has been the dominant practice—until recently. Traditional Islam has considered cremation an "unclean practice," and

Islamic leaders today will still remind their followers, "We believe that God gave us this body as a trust. We must take care of it before and after death. Since he put us in a full body on earth, we must return to God in a full body. We want to return to him in the best way possible."[3] In Judaism, leaders remind adherents that "Jewish law mandates that human remains be buried after death" and this is why burial has been a dominant practice among Jewish people for millennia.[4] Yet, as is the case with those who confess Christianity, the cremation of deceased Jewish people is on the rise.

In America it has been reported by the National Funeral Directors Association that for the first time in our country's history, cremations are performed more than 50 percent of the time and are expected to near 80 percent by the year 2035. In Canada, the number will rise to 90 percent by that same time.[5] Commentators are quick to tie this departure from the Christian, Jewish, and Islamic practice to an overall departure from religion in America.[6] Even practicing Roman Catholics have felt increasing freedom to cremate the bodies of their loved ones after the Vatican, in 2016, gave allowance for it as long as the ashes are buried and not scattered.[7]

The acceleration of this trend toward cremation—in America in particular—has been phenomenal: from under 10 percent in 1980 to more than 25 percent in 2001 to more than half today.[8] As Christians in the midst of this seismic shift, it is important for us to give this topic some careful thought with Scripture in mind. Most churchgoers today hold to the societal norm, which is basically, "What happens to my body after I die doesn't matter." Is that truly the case? Let's take time to understand why burial was the biblical pattern.

WHY BURIAL HAS MATTERED TO CHRISTIANS

In the Bible, burial is depicted as the practice of respectfully laying a deceased human body in the ground, a cave, or a sepulcher to await its reconstitution and resurrection. Now, as many people have rightly noted, biblical references to burial are *descriptive* rather than *prescriptive*.[9] There is no express command as to how to deal with a body when one dies. But we should at least attempt to understand what motivated this practice, and make sure that we don't depart from this consistent biblical pattern without thinking through the matter very carefully.

The Human Body Has Intrinsic Value

As beings who were created to exist as both body and spirit, the body has always been held in high honor in the Scripture. Human biological anatomy was initially designed and personally crafted by God himself (Genesis 2:7). Each individual body ever since has been understood in the Bible to be sovereignly fashioned by God. As David expressed in praise to God, "you formed my inward parts; you knitted me together in my mother's womb. I praise you, for I am fearfully and wonderfully made. Wonderful are your works; my soul knows it very well" (Psalm 139:13-14). The wonderful works of the human body and soul are presented to us as the pinnacle of God's physical creation (Psalm 8).

During our lifetime, we as Christians are called to have a special care and concern for our physical bodies. Even certain sins are highlighted as having an undignified impact on our bodies.

> Flee from sexual immorality. Every other sin a person commits is outside the body, but the sexually immoral person sins against his own body. Or do you not know that your body is a temple of the Holy Spirit within you, whom you have from God? You are not your own, for you were bought with a price. So glorify God in your body (1 Corinthians 6:18-20).

Our bodies are described as sacred vessels that house not only our own spirit but, if we are Christians, they house the Holy Spirit himself. Of course, this is changed at the moment of death (as we examined in chapter 2). We are separated from our bodies when we die (Genesis 35:18; Acts 7:59; James 2:26). But that is not the end of the story for our human bodies.

God Is Not Done with Our Bodies Yet

As we considered in chapter 4, God's authoritative promise for our body is that it will follow the pattern of Christ's: "Christ has been raised from the dead, the firstfruits of those who have fallen asleep" (1 Corinthians 15:20). He will "transform our lowly body to be like his glorious body" (Philippians 3:21).

In the same way that Jesus's body went into the tomb and was raised, our bodies will be raised. Yes, they will be transformed, but just as the tomb was empty because God raised the same body that went in, transforming and glorifying it, so it will be with our bodies. For Christ, it took place on the third day. For us, the timing is unknown. It might be on the third day, the three-hundredth day, or the three-thousandth day. Whatever the case, God has promised to raise our bodies in the same way he raised Christ's.

Suppose you had been present when Christ spoke these words, and you had clearly understood what he meant at the time:

> Jesus answered them, "Destroy this temple, and in three days I will raise it up." The Jews then said, "It has taken forty-six years to build this temple, and will you raise it up in three days?" But he was speaking about the temple of his body. When therefore he was raised from the dead, his disciples remembered that he had said this, and they believed the Scripture and the word that Jesus had spoken (John 2:19-22).

If this were your anticipation as you were helping to take Jesus's deceased body off of the cross, I wonder what kind of "disposal" of his body you would be in favor of? I assume you would not even speak in such terms! You wouldn't want to "dispose" of it; rather, you would want to do what we find throughout the Bible: You would choose to respectfully lay it in the ground to await its reconstitution and resurrection. I believe we would all intuitively vote against burning his body or pulverizing it. I doubt we would shrug our shoulders and say, "It doesn't matter what happens to his body. He will get a new one."

If you truly understood the promise of the resurrection, you wouldn't even speak in terms of a "new" body. You might rightly talk of a glorified or transformed body, but you would expect a correspondence between the body that goes in the grave, cave, crypt, tomb, or sepulcher and the one that has been promised to come out.

In response to that line of reasoning, many have said to me, "Well, my body is just going to turn to dust anyway. Why not cremate it and let it become dust right away? Isn't that what God said about dead bodies in Genesis 3:19?" Yes, God spoke of Adam being made from the dust and said "to dust you shall return." But knowing the body is made from the material of earth and committing the body back to the material of earth does not negate the biblical anticipation we should all eagerly await—specifically, that "many of those who sleep in the dust of the earth shall awake, some to everlasting life" (Daniel 12:2).

You may respectfully bury your Christian loved one's body awaiting this promised day, and many centuries could conceivably pass until this resurrection physically takes place. But, then again, it might be a few short years, a couple of months, or even a handful of days. Either way, knowing that God has promised to reconstitute what is left of decomposing bodies should be enough for us to understand why the biblical pattern was consistent: Christians buried the deceased bodies of their loved ones.

Dead Bodies Mattered

There are numerous biblical examples of the amount of care that was given to the bodies of the deceased. Consider Sarah, Abraham,

Deborah, Isaac, Jacob, Joseph, Aaron, Moses, and many others—including Jesus Christ. There was care given to finding a proper place to lay the body. There was interest in the preservation methods—some simple, and some elaborate. There was anxiety when a body was not properly accounted for. In the one example we have of an important figure in Israel being burned (seemingly out of necessity), we see that the distress was great for the people of God to retrieve what was left of King Saul's body and to bury his bones in a respectful place (1 Samuel 31:8-13).

For those who suggest, "It doesn't matter what happens to my body or my loved one's body when the spirit is gone," consider the many laws, even in our modern society, regarding the desecration of the dead. This is not just a health concern. Most states and municipalities have stringent laws pertaining to what people can and cannot do to a corpse. There are an abundance of laws prohibiting necrophilia, as well as the desecration, mutilation, profaning, or defiling of a dead body. Certainly, these societal rules reflect our intuitive and collective conscience that the body does in fact matter, even after a person is dead.

Many years ago, knowing that the pastoral team at my church was often consulted about choices regarding burial or cremation, I took the unpleasant step of taking these leaders to see as much of both processes as we were allowed. I considered it important to be informed about what we were recommending when we said one thing or the other. I called some contacts I knew in the field and was able to get a behind-the-scenes tour at one of the largest funeral providers in the country. It was a memorable afternoon. They showed us much of what is involved in both cremation and in the preparation for burial. Without going into details, I believe our pastoral team was impacted by what they learned—things they might not otherwise have considered when giving this kind of counsel and helping people make these sorts of choices.

I know most of us would rather not think about this subject at all. But when we weigh the values and practices of Scripture with an informed knowledge of the options available to us in our day, wisdom tends to emerge in favor of the biblical practice.

In my reading on the topic, I suspect that a significant reason for the rise of cremation in Western society is the increasing tendency of people to sweep the prospects of the afterlife under the carpet. There are many moderns who say, "You go around once in life, and then it's over." Cremation, at least for some, is their exclamation that says, "It's over!...I hope." Yet the Bible reminds us that while the non-Christian world is subject to lifelong slavery through the fear of death, we have not only been freed from that enslavement, but have had the sting of death removed (1 Corinthians 15:55; Hebrews 2:14-15). For us "to live is Christ, and to die is gain" (Philippians 1:21). Our great confidence and hope is the resurrection from the dead (Philippians 3:11)

Dignified Burials Were Important

It is uncontested that burial is the biblical pattern. Beyond that, however, we should take notice of the dignity associated with the proper burial of a loved one as compared to the disdain that is associated with those who were not honorably interned:

> If a man fathers a hundred children and lives many years, so that the days of his years are many, but his soul is not satisfied with life's good things, and he also has no burial, I say that a stillborn child is better off than he (Ecclesiastes 6:3).

Old Testament scholars who comment on this passage explain that burial was highly valued and was a sign of proper respect for the deceased. For a person to not receive a burial was a "deep humiliation," a mark of being despised or not properly mourned.[10] This contrast is made when the bodies of the former kings of the ancient

Near East are described as "lying in glory" compared to the shame that is prophesied for the king of Babylon:

> All the kings of the nations lie in glory, each in his own tomb; but you are cast out, away from your grave, like a loathed branch, clothed with the slain, those pierced by the sword, who go down to the stones of the pit, like a dead body trampled underfoot. You will not be joined with them in burial, because you have destroyed your land, you have slain your people (Isaiah 14:18-20).

This disgrace is strongly communicated in other passages of Scripture with regard to those who are not properly buried. Jeremiah prophesied with great pain over the desecration of the tombs of the kings of Judah, saying their bones would be dragged out of their sepulchers and "shall not be gathered or buried. They shall be as dung on the surface of the ground" (Jeremiah 8:2). Later he foretold of the coming end of the bloodthirsty and oppressive King Jehoiakim, saying, "With the burial of a donkey he shall be buried, dragged and dumped beyond the gates of Jerusalem" (Jeremiah 22:19). And Elisha delivered these words from God regarding the death of the infamously evil Queen Jezebel: "The dogs shall eat Jezebel in the territory of Jezreel, and none shall bury her" (2 Kings 9:10).

ISN'T BURIAL JUST A CULTURAL PRACTICE?

There are plenty of cultural aspects to precisely how God's people buried or interred the deceased in the ancient Near East or Greco-Roman contexts. But the basic idea of respectfully laying aside a deceased human body in the ground, a cave, or a sepulcher to await its reconstitution and resurrection was clearly driven by theology, not culture. Even in ancient and modern Hinduism there may be distinctions between the specific features associated with the burning of bodies, but the general motivation to burn the bodies of their loved ones is driven by their core religious beliefs regarding the body, the spirit, and their understanding of reincarnation and the afterlife.

As I have suggested, I am convinced through my research that the growing acceptance of cremation in Western culture reflects an increasingly widespread expression of secular beliefs about life, death, and the afterlife. I, of course, am not saying that everyone who has their loved one's bodies buried or burned is expressing their philosophical worldview or making a statement for or against God's promise of the resurrection. But, as I attempted to do in this chapter, I do say that it would be wise for us as Christians to give thought about the connection between our practices and our theology.

Because my pastoral counsel on this matter is assembled from the principles and practices of the Bible and is not any express command in a "chapter and verse," I cannot say with any biblical authority that those who choose to cremate are choosing to do something sinful. Again, my goal here is to get Christians to think more deeply about the matter. I have discovered, over my decades of ministry to God's people, that most in the Christian community have not given this matter much consideration at all—at least, not in light of their theology. As one theologian rightly put it:

> It's a matter of Christian judgment and an understanding of the fact that burial has had very deep theological and biblical roots in the Christian and in the Jewish tradition. And it's because of a reverence for and respect for the body—it's described in the New Testament for Christians as the temple of the Holy Spirit. And furthermore, there's been a respect for the body that has stood in distinction to the spiritual and theological beliefs of other cultures that have practiced cremation.[11]

CAN'T GOD RESURRECT ASHES?

Yes, God can resurrect ashes. He can reassemble any atomic particles from any corner of the vast created universe over which he exercises complete sovereignty. There is no doubt about this. If someone's body was lost at sea, eaten by wild beasts in the forest, or consumed in a fiery car crash on some remote country road, God would have no difficulty reconstituting and resurrecting that body. We can rest assured that if we have chosen to have a loved one cremated, our decision will not imperil our loved one's future resurrection.

While that can give assurance with regard to any past decisions made about deceased bodies, I wouldn't advise utilizing the logic that "God can" as reason for deciding to break with the biblical pattern of burial. When I speak of respectful burial, I mean that in two ways: You are not only showing respect for the person's body, you are also showing respect for God.

Again, God can reconstitute and resurrect a body no matter what condition it is in. But there is something respectful about not reducing a body to ashes under the assumption it will probably reach that state anyway. As I said earlier, we have no idea when the resurrection will take place. Scripture calls us to live in light of Christ's imminent return, and I am unwilling to concede the point that cremation does nothing but expedite the process that will take place anyway, and as long as we know God is able to raise a person's remains no matter what, why not?[12]

When my kids were young and they broke a toy, they would take it out to the garage and set it on my workbench to await my arrival home from work. They were sure I could fix it. Let's imagine they bragged to other kids about my great skill at repairing their beloved knickknacks. I would have been honored to hear such things, but I wouldn't have taken that as a compliment if they were purposely smashing and destroying their toys just because they knew I could fix them. I had gifted those toys to them, and I wanted them to take care of them. When they were broken (as I knew they would eventually be), I wanted my kids to show honor for the toys *and their dad* by respectfully laying aside these broken items until I came home to repair them.

> *The biblical practice of laying aside a deceased body in anticipation of the Lord's promise of the resurrection is a display of respect for both the deceased and God.*

Being motivated to cremate because "God can restore the ashes" would be like the wedding guests at Cana pouring water out of the jars just before Jesus turned the water into wine because they had confidence he could do his miracle even if the water was spilled out on the ground. I have no doubt Jesus could pull all hydrogen and oxygen atoms out of the soil so he could create the complex chemical compounds that are present in wine. Even so, I don't believe the guests' actions would have been taken as a compliment. That is why I believe the biblical practice of laying aside a deceased body in anticipation of the Lord's promise of the resurrection is a display of respect for both the deceased and God.

BUT CREMATION IS
ECONOMICAL AND ECOLOGICAL

I can't argue with the fact that cremation is more affordable than burial. It is. But we shouldn't make our decisions, as Christians, based on what costs less. Not that every internment has to be elaborate or exorbitant. I have officiated many dignified and respectful burials with low-cost caskets in tax-supported county cemeteries. Consumer protection is on the rise in the funeral industry, and the price-gouging that unfortunately has characterized some businesses in this industry is easier for us to avoid these days.

Not only have I witnessed some respectful yet economical burials, our church has often pulled together funds for needy families so they can underwrite the costs associated with purchasing a casket and a burial plot. I'm sure our church is not alone. This is what the people of God do when others in our flock are grieving and in need.

I have read alarmists who advocate cremation because we are quickly running out of room on our crowded planet to bury our dead. They are concerned about space, and some even find rare anecdotes about the biological threat that burial causes. Well, we should all be in favor of the proper management of graveyards and cemeteries. And with rare exceptions, they are well maintained. Like all industries, there will be occasional stories of misconduct and mismanagement, but I don't believe there is evidence that the funeral industry is a threat to the health and welfare of the inhabitants of earth.

As for running out of room to bury people, every time I sit at a window seat on a cross-country flight, I am reminded how much space there is on this planet. My musings about squeezing in an old-fashioned churchyard out in front of every church building in the crowded cities may be unrealistic, but I don't think the master planning of new communities, or the expanded development of the fringes of old communities, would in any way truly preclude appropriate space for burying our dead. We seem to find plenty of acres of property for just about every frivolous endeavor of the modern age. And even if we have to drive to the remotest parts of our counties because our culture wants to sweep the reminders of death out of sight, I believe we as Christians would do well to make the trek and intern our loved ones.

Advance planning for your own burial is always wise regardless of where you live. To buy a plot and prepay some of the arrangements is a preparation for eventualities that, barring the return of

Christ in your lifetime, is more certain than anything else you've put on your calendar.

WHAT ABOUT ORGAN DONATION?

Since the reason I would choose to have my body respectfully laid aside when I die is because God is going to resurrect it, I am often asked, "Then what about organ donation?"

There a drastic difference between what I would argue is the unnecessary burning and pulverizing of the human body, and the act of giving a bodily organ for the good of someone else. As I have affirmed throughout this chapter and this book, God will reconstitute, resurrect, and glorify our bodies by an exertion of his power—a kind of power that enables him to subject all things to himself (Philippians 3:21). No daunting problem exists for God regarding those who enter life missing a hand, a leg, or an eye, as Jesus said in Matthew 18:8-9. God will take the glorified blueprint of that individual, assemble whatever material is necessary, and craft the perfect hand, leg, or eye for those people.

The act of gifting a part of one's body for someone else is an act that in no way imperils one's "whole" resurrection. As with the Christians eaten by lions or burned at the stake, we can fully expect that the resurrected and glorified bodies of Christian organ donors will be whole and fully functioning.

The technology to do organ transplants was obviously not available to those in the New Testament era, but that doesn't mean the desire for such technology didn't exist. For example, the apostle Paul had some sort of ailment that severely affected his eyesight. At one point, he said of those who dearly loved him, "I testify to you that, if possible, you would have gouged out your eyes and given them to me" (Galatians 4:15). I am sure that if Paul's ailment had been kidney failure, liver disease, or a shutdown of his pancreas, and the technology for organ transplants had existed during the first century

AD, many would have stepped up to donate a kidney or a segment of their liver or pancreas. I believe this would have been, or is now, a well-pleasing sacrifice from God's point of view. It is a measurable expression of the kind of sacrificial love Jesus taught us to exercise (John 15:13; 1 John 3:16-18).

The same is true about postmortem organ donations. Caution and wisdom need to be prayerfully and thoughtfully applied to these decisions because of the end-of-life concerns that are associated with the harvesting of organs. When it comes to gifting bodily organs, we must not sacrifice the biblical priority of the sanctity and preservation of life of the dying. We cannot, as Christians, support the purposeful acceleration or termination of life so that organs can be harvested. But barring these concerns, postmortem organ donation does not interfere with the theology of Christian burial.

THE MODERN FUNERAL SERVICE

As long as we are on this unpleasant topic of death, let me close with a quick word about funeral services. With the exception of funeral directors, it is fair to say that we pastors attend more funerals than anyone else. We see them all the time—not from the back row, but from the platform. We are not passive bystanders, but active participants in helping families through the grieving process, speaking at the services and gravesides, and counseling people in the aftermath. While I am not the first to make the following observations, from my pastoral vantage point, I want to join those Christian leaders who are concerned with the changes we've witnessed over the decades in the ways that families and friends of the deceased want the services to be conducted.[13] And because a portion of the funeral service is generally conducted by family and friends who rightly prepare to eulogize their loved one, much of the tone of the gathering is set and directed by them.

The trend to "celebrate life" instead of mourning the loss of the relationship and give sober thought to the seriousness of death is, I believe, another example of trying to avoid the serious theological issues we are all appropriately intended to consider when a loved one dies. When jokes and vacation stories are the norm, and laughter is the goal of every eulogy, we have missed something profound and certainly intended by God in these serious settings. The Bible says, "It is better to go to the house of mourning than to go to the house of feasting, for this is the end of all mankind, and the living will lay it to heart" (Ecclesiastes 7:2). A "house of mourning" rarely exists these days. I would venture to say few people have ever "gone" to one, even if they have been to several funerals.

While I am not advocating some display of grandiose lamentation or insincere wailing, I am asking that we take a good look at the painful problem death actually is—theologically and personally. We would do well to rethink our approach to funerals and consider whether we are not trying to avoid what is right in front of us. The Bible says the living need to take this reality "to heart." Unfortunately, we will never get there if our songs, slideshows, and scripts are all designed to make us laugh and evade the seriousness of death.

This is not to say that we need to grieve as those who have no hope (1 Thessalonians 4:13). As Christians, we do have hope. An incredible hope that this "last enemy," as the Bible calls it, has lost its ultimate power over us (1 Corinthians 15:26). But we grieve. We grieve as Christ did at the death of his friend Lazarus. "Jesus wept" (John 11:35), even though the resuscitation of his loved one was minutes away. Thankfully, the Christ who wept at a funeral was also the Christ who said at the funeral, "I am the resurrection and the life. Whoever believes in me, though he die, yet shall he live" (verse 25). In the end, He will "wipe away every tear," and "death shall be no more" (Revelation 21:4). In this we rejoice, "though now for a little while" we are "grieved by various trials" (1 Peter 1:6)—the most serious of which is death.

But thanks be to God that

> Jesus died and rose again, even so, through Jesus, God will bring with him those who have fallen asleep. For this we declare to you by a word from the Lord, that we who are alive, who are left until the coming of the Lord, will not precede those who have fallen asleep. For the Lord himself will descend from heaven with a cry of command, with the voice of an archangel, and with the sound of the trumpet of God. And the dead in Christ will rise first. Then we who are alive, who are left, will be caught up together with them in the clouds to meet the Lord in the air, and so we will always be with the Lord. Therefore encourage one another with these words (1 Thessalonians 4:14-18).

Becoming a Christian

Being prepared for the afterlife ought to be everyone's serious concern. Thankfully, God has given us clear instruction as to how we can be fully qualified for his coming kingdom, and have our appointment at the Great White Throne of his justice canceled once and for all.

THE FOUNDATIONAL INFORMATION

Before we can jump into the good news of the New Testament gospel, we must be careful to process the indispensable prologue that God set forth in the Old Testament.

1. God Is Our Creator

The Bible begins with the declaration that God is the originator of all things. And as such, God is our authority. He is in charge. By virtue of his position as our Creator, he is the One to whom we, his creatures, must give an account. This may be a hard truth for the independent, freedom-loving, twenty-first-century human to accept, but this is where all Christian theology begins—God is the owner, rule-maker, and sovereign over each one of us.

2. God Is Holy

The Bible goes to great lengths to describe the absolute perfection of God. He is presented to us as morally and personally perfect in all that he is and does. The Lord himself is the standard of everything that can be described as good or right. While some of God's attributes (such as his unrestricted power and his ability to be aware of all things in all places) cannot be shared by any of his creatures, many aspects of his nature become the reasonable and expected standard for each of us. For example, like him, we should be loving, truthful, and faithful.

3. We Are Sinful and Separated from God

The problem, of course, is that we are not holy in all of our behavior. We are quick to identify the moral imperfection of those around us, and if we are honest, we should be able to readily admit that we ourselves have fallen short of the standard of God's holiness. While we could itemize a million negative consequences of this human sinfulness, the biggest consequence is that we are left separated from God. And because human sin stretches all the way back to Adam, we, as the human race, are all alienated from the perfect God who made us. While it is true that his goodness is undeservedly experienced in a number of ways, the fact remains that due to our sin we are not able to have the fellowship and the blessings we were created to experience with our Creator.

4. God Is Just

In chapter after chapter the Bible demonstrates that God is just. His justice is an expression of his perfection. In the same way a local judge in our county could not be a "good judge" if he gave a pass to every criminal that was hauled in before his tribunal, so God would sacrifice his perfection if he rewarded sinners as though they were righteous. God is a just God who must resolve the inequity that exists when wrongs are committed against his holy standard.

5. We Deserve God's Punishment

The awful reality of coming to grips with our status as sinners is that we come to realize that there must be an ultimate accountability for all of our sinful thoughts, words, and actions. Because God has personally provided us the proper standard for our lives, and because our rebellion against that standard is a snubbing of him, the deserved punishment is much greater than most ever consider. Just as an angry act of rebellion against a coworker would justly require one degree of consequence, and an angry act of rebellion against the CEO would require another degree of consequence, our sins, which are ultimately against God, demand the most serious punishment of all.

6. God Is Loving

Up to this point, the picture painted by Scripture is a disheartening one. But thankfully, the Bible breaks through with hope for sinners. God reveals himself to be a loving God. His love is unparalleled. God, we are told, is so kindly committed to the well-being of his creatures that he has reached out to solve our ultimate problem at great personal cost to himself. In light of God's intrinsic authority, holiness, and justice, he could, without any violation of his character, have decided to condemn the entire lot of his creatures to the just penalty for their sins. Thankfully, because of God's incredible love, he has provided a solution.

THE GOSPEL

The "good news" of God's solution for our dilemma is all about Jesus Christ. From Genesis to Revelation, the story of God's redemptive work on behalf of sinners has been symbolized, narrated, prophesied, demonstrated, and explained as the story of Jesus coming to save sinners from the penalty of and enslavement to their sins.

1. Jesus Is God

It becomes clear, early on in the Bible, that only God himself is capable of solving the human problem. Sinful people are incapable of drawing themselves out of their sins or doing some sort of absolving work to compensate for their transgressions. In the New Testament, Jesus steps into time and space as the second Person of the Triune God to live as a participant of humanity in order to fulfill all the holy requirements of human righteousness. His status as the God-man not only secures success as the absolutely perfect human life, but it also makes the value of his death capable of being applied to millions of people.

2. Jesus Lived and Died as Our Substitute

Beginning with the early instructions of Old Testament worship, the requirement for a substitute was made clear. If we as sinners are to be gifted the blessings of life and fellowship with God, someone else must incur the penalty we deserve. While the sacrifices of spotless animals couldn't actually transact our forgiveness, it was a powerful symbolic image of the substitution that was needed. The perfect would need to be accepted as the substitute for the sinful. Christ came to live the life we should have lived so that it could be credited to us. More than that, Christ came to suffer the judgment for sin that we deserve so that we could be treated by God as though we had lived his sinless life.

3. Jesus Conquered Death for Us

The result of this work of Christ enabled God to justly set us free from the penalty of our sin. That penalty included both relational death (that is, broken fellowship with God) and biological death (that is, the permanent destruction of our bodies). With God's justice being fully satisfied by the life and death of Christ, he demonstrated the reversal of the sentence of death by biologically raising Christ from the dead. Christ's resurrection powerfully confirmed that he took care of our sin problem, and we can be assured that he will also take care of the problem of death. The historical proof of Christ's victory over death proved that our sins had also been completely defeated, and became a major triumphal theme in the pages of the New Testament.

THE CALL OF THE GOSPEL

While all of the redemptive work was accomplished by Christ in history, its benefits are applied now to individuals as they respond appropriately to the message of the gospel. The Bible repeatedly calls each person to respond to this good news in two distinct yet inseparable ways.

1. Repentance

God commands everyone to repent of their sins. Repentance is more than simply changing one's mind about who Christ is, or agreeing to the facts regarding what Christ has done. Repentance goes further and involves a realization that one's sins are the profound problem that required the life and death of Christ as the only adequate solution. It includes a repudiation or renunciation of thoughts, words, and actions that fall short of God's holy standard. It is, in short, an internal conclusion that one is now turning from sin to God.

2. Faith

God calls us all to place our faith in Christ and his finished work on our behalf. Faith is depicted in the Bible as more than assenting to a set of facts or agreeing to a list of religious beliefs. Faith is the internal transfer of our trust away from anything we have done or could do to become acceptable before God, and instead placing our complete confidence in Jesus as the One who has done all that is required for us to be made right with our Creator.

THE FRUIT OF THE GOSPEL

A genuine response of repentance and faith is a work of God that will always result in a changed life. There are at least four results one can expect to see when someone turns from sin and trusts in Christ.

1. New Godly Desires

The Bible tells us that real Christians are made new from the inside out. A transformation takes place enlivening us to God and his will. As Christians we can begin to see this clearly when we contemplate our core desires. These ultimate longings will shift from the selfish impulses of a fallen heart to the Godward longings of loving and wanting to please our Maker. During this life our fallen human bodies will still crave many sinful things, but our new core desires will strongly object to those old fleshly desires. This clash of cravings is normal for Christians and will last until we receive our resurrected bodies.

2. Curbed Sinful Habits

This battle against sin is intense, but the Bible assures us that transformative progress will be made. Between now and the future redemption of our bodies, incremental victory will be won as our core desires, aided and empowered by God's Spirit, fight day by day to prevail. The old enslavement to sinful habits will be increasingly broken as we grow up in our Christian lives. These changes will be noticeable to those who observe our lives. The people we once were, before God granted us new life, will become less and less perceptible.

3. Righteous Deeds

As our new lives are fueled by God's Spirit and the truth from the Bible, we will find that our Christian lives are characterized by more than just avoiding sinful actions. We will quickly discover a powerful thirst to do the righteous things God has asked us to do in his Word. A variety of practices, habits, and conversations that honor Christ and bring glory to God will progressively define who we are. People will inevitably see a growing set of biblical good deeds and godly wisdom that never characterized our lives before we became Christians.

4. Lifelong Discipleship

The Bible frequently warns of a counterfeit Christianity that may initially look like real Christianity but will prove to be otherwise as any fervor for Christ and his Word gives way to the old way of life. Instead of being transformed from the inside out by God's Spirit, counterfeit Christians are those who for a time simply conform to a Christian standard of behavior or practice on the outside. Evidence of genuine repentance and faith is revealed when a person's love and obedience to Christ, with all of its highs and lows, lasts for a lifetime.

Notes

WHAT LIES BEYOND THE GRAVE?

1. George Bernard Shaw, as cited in "The Great Spoiler" in *Discipleship Journal*, Issue 19 (January/February 1984).

2. Linda Sunshine, ed., *The Illustrated Woody Allen Reader* (New York: Alfred A. Knopf, 1993), p. 250.

3. William Shakespeare, "The Plays and Sonnets," *Encyclopedia Britannica*, vol. 25 (London: Encyclopedia Britannica, Inc., 1990), p. 47.

4. Paul P. Enns, *The Moody Handbook of Theology* (Chicago: Moody Press, 1989), p. 168.

5. See, for instance, Josh McDowell's *Evidence that Demands a Verdict* (Nashville, TN: Thomas Nelson, 1999); Walt Kaiser's *Messiah in the Old Testament* (Wheaton, IL: Zondervan, 1995); or Barton Payne's *Encyclopedia of Biblical Prophecy* (Grand Rapids, MI: Baker Books, 1980).

6. Wilbur M. Smith, *The Incomparable Book* (CreateSpace, 2015), Kindle Edition, pp. 5-6.

7. John Foxe, *Foxe's Book of Martyrs* (Philadelphia, PA: The John C. Winston Co., 1926), pp. 1-6.

8. Chuck Colson, http://archive.breakpoint.org/bpcommentaries/entry/13/12231.

CHAPTER 1—ALL ROADS LEAD TO HEAVEN

1. John Hick, *God Has Many Names* (Westminster: John Oxford Press, 1982), p. 19.

2. D. James Kennedy, *Evangelism Explosion* (Wheaton, IL: Tyndale House, 1970), p. 22.

3. "Harry Randall Truman," https://en.wikipedia.org/wiki/Harry_Randall_Truman.

4. William Ernest Henley, "Invictus," Poetry Foundation, https://www.poetryfoundation.org/poems/51642/invictus.

CHAPTER 2—WHEN I DIE I'LL GO TO SLEEP UNTIL THE RESURRECTION

1. "Heaven Tourism," Challies, https://www.challies.com/articles/heaven-tourism/; and "A Modern History of Heaven Tourism," Challies, https://www.challies.com/articles/greetings-from-heaven-a-modern-history-of-heaven-tourism/.

2. Ron Rhodes, *The Wonder of Heaven* (Eugene, OR: Harvest House Publishers, 2009), pp. 239-244.

3. T.J. Demy and Thomas Ice, *Answers to Common Questions About Heaven and Eternity* (Grand Rapids, MI: Kregel, 2011), pp. 63-65.

4. John MacArthur, *The Glory of Heaven* (Wheaton, IL: Crossway Books, 1996), p. 13.

5. John Weldon, *The Facts on Life After Death* (Chattanooga, TN: ATRI Publishing), Kindle locations 208-209.

6. J.B. Polhill, *Paul and His Letters* (Nashville, TN: Broadman & Holman, 1999), p. 250.

7. "This doctrine is one of the distinctive tenets of Jehovah's Witnesses, and also of the Seventh-day Adventists."…Berkhof says: "Eusebius makes mention of a small sect in Arabia that held this view. During the Middle Ages there were quite a few so-called Psychopannychians, and at the time of the Reformation this error was advocated by some of the Anabaptists…In the nineteenth century this doctrine was held by some of the Irvingites in England, and in our day it is one of the favorite doctrines of the Russellites or Millennial Dawnists of our own country." Loraine Boettner, *Immortality* (Phillipsburg, NJ: Presbyterian & Reformed, 1956), p. 109.

8. The English translation, "Truly, I say to you today, you will be…" is only possible with a rearrangement of the Greek sentence (i.e., "I say today to you"), which is found only in the Curetonian Syriac manuscript of the Gospel of Luke and stands against the evidence of a multitude of ancient Greek manuscripts. See B.M. Metzger, *A Textual Commentary on The Greek New Testament*, 4th rev. ed. (Stuttgart: United Bible Societies, 1994), p. 155. This singular evidence of an ancient rearrangement was, according to scholar Joseph A. Fitzmyer, inserted because of a community's preexisting eschatological beliefs and not because of the textual evidence. Fitzmyer, *Luke X–XXIV* (New Haven: Yale University Press, 2008), p. 1510; as cited by J.R. Edwards, *The Gospel According to Luke*, D.A. Carson, ed. (Grand Rapids, MI: Eerdmans, 2015).

CHAPTER 3—ON MY WAY TO HEAVEN I'LL HAVE TO PUT IN SOME TIME IN PURGATORY

1. "How many Roman Catholics are there in the world?" BBC News, March 14, 2013, http://www .bbc.com/news/world-21443313.

2. Approximately 81.6 million Americans claim to be Roman Catholic—"Catholicism in the US," *Wall Street Journal*, September 18, 2015, http://graphics.wsj.com/catholics-us/.

3. See section 1427 of the *Catechism of the Catholic Church*, 2d ed. (Washington, DC: United States Catholic Conference, 2000).

4. W.E. Addis and T. Arnold, *A Catholic Dictionary*, 6th ed. (New York: The Catholic Publication Society, 1887), p. 702.

5. *Catechism of the Catholic Church*, 2d ed. (Washington, DC: United States Catholic Conference, 2000), §882, p. 234.

6. *Catechism*, §95 p. 29.

7. *Catechism*, p. 901.

8. As many are aware, the Roman Catholics authorized an additional set of books known as the *deuterocanonicals* (i.e., the "second canon," more popularly known as the Apocrypha) at the Council

of Trent during the counter-Reformation of the sixteenth century. This small collection of inter-testamental books and additions to existing Old Testament books were "authorized" by the Roman Catholic Church for the sake of two primary passages in the narrative of the Maccabean revolt that, in their view, propped up their side of the Reformation contention that the Church was selling indulgences. For a concise explanation on why these books are not marked by signs of divine inspiration, see "The Apocryphal Books" in Neil R. Lightfoot's *How We Got the Bible* (Grand Rapids, MI: Baker, 2010).

9. *Catechism*, p. 887.

10. *Catechism*, §889, p. 235.

11. *Catechism*, §891, pp. 235-236.

12. "The Catholic Difference" in *Evangelicals and Catholics Together*, eds. Charles Colson and Richard John Neuhaus (Dallas, TX: Word, 1995), p. 216.

13. Pope Benedict XVI, Joseph Ratzinger in *Communio*, Volume 1 (Grand Rapids, MI: Eerdmans, 2010), pp. 73-74.

14. *Catechism*, §1031, p. 268.

15. *Catechism*, §1472, p. 370.

16. *Catechism*, §1030, p. 268.

17. The glossary of *Catechism of the Catholic Church* defines *penance* as acts that "include fasting, prayer, and almsgiving" and the "observance of certain penitential practices" (p. 892). §1461 of the *Catechism*—which deals with penance—explains that "since Christ entrusted to his apostles the ministry of reconciliation, bishops who are their successors, and priests, the bishops' collaborators, continue to exercise this ministry. Indeed bishops and priests, by virtue of the sacrament of Holy Orders, have the power to forgive all sins 'in the name of the Father, and of the Son, and of the Holy Spirit'" (p. 367).

18. §1471 of the *Catechism* says, "An indulgence is a remission before God of the temporal punishment due to sins whose guilt has already been forgiven, which the faithful Christian who is duly disposed gains under certain prescribed conditions through the action of the Church which, as the minister of redemption, dispenses and applies with authority the treasury of the satisfactions of Christ and the saints. An indulgence is partial or plenary according as it removes either part or all of the temporal punishment due to sin. The faithful can gain indulgences for themselves or apply them to the dead" (p. 370).

19. Tony Lane, "A Man for All People: Introducing William Tyndale," *Christian History*, Issue 16, 1987.

20. Horatio Spafford, "It Is Well with My Soul," 1873.

CHAPTER 4—HEAVEN IS FILLED WITH SEE-THROUGH BODIES AND COTTON-BALL CLOUDS

1. "Mark Twain and Bermuda," *Bermuda Online*, http://www.bermuda-online.org/twain.htm.

2. Twain Quotes, http://www.twainquotes.com/Heaven.html.

3. "Twain Scholar to Speak on American Author," *The Royal Gazette*, http://www.royalgazette.com/article/20151102/ISLAND04/151109992.

4. R.L. Thomas, *Revelation 8–22* (Chicago: Moody, 1995), p. 439.

5. W. Arndt, F.W. Danker, W. Bauer, and F.W. Gingrich, *A Greek-English Lexicon of the New Testament and Other Early Christian Literature*, 3d ed. (Chicago: University of Chicago Press, 2000), p. 587.

6. See Randy Alcorn's book *Heaven* (Wheaton, IL: Tyndale House, 2011) or Joni Eareckson Tada's encouraging book *Heaven: Your Real Home* (Grand Rapids, MI: Zondervan, 1995) for starters.

CHAPTER 5—HEAVEN IS FILLED WITH TRACT HOMES AND GOVERNMENT-ISSUED UNIFORMS

1. W.A. Grudem, *Politics According to the Bible* (Grand Rapids, MI: Zondervan, 2010), p. 262.

2. William Carey, "The Missionary Herald" in *The Baptist Magazine*, vol. 35, January 1843, p. 41.

3. Quoted in William R. Moody's *The Life of Dwight L. Moody* (New York: Fleming H. Revell, 1900), p. 541.

4. C.S. Lewis, *The Weight of Glory* (New York: HarperCollins, 2015) Kindle edition, p. 27.

5. John Wesley, *Explanatory Notes Upon the New Testament* (New York: Lane & Tippett, 1847), p. 676.

6. For instance, see Wayne Grudem's *Business for the Glory of God* (Wheaton, IL: Crossway Books, 2003).

CHAPTER 6—I'M AFRAID I MIGHT SIN MY WAY OUT OF HEAVEN

1. John Murray, *Redemption* (Grand Rapids, MI: William B. Eerdmans, 1955), p. 175.

2. See "The Names of Satan" (pp. 127-133) and "Satan's Present Power and Activity" (pp. 151-159) in C. Fred Dickason's *Angels: Elect & Evil* (Chicago: Moody Press, 1995).

3. Martin Luther, "A Mighty Fortress Is Our God," c. 1527.

4. "What's the Word?" *WELS Hymnal Project,* http://welshymnal.com/blog/whats-word.

5. See Matthew Waymeyer's coverage of this important feature of the end times in *Revelation 20 and the Millennial Debate* (Woodlands, TX: Kress Christian Publications, 2004).

6. For more on these events, see Mark Hitchcock, *The End: A Complete Overview of Bible Prophecy and the End of Days* (Carol Stream, IL: Tyndale House, 2012); Michael J. Vlach, *Premillennialism: Why There Must Be a Future Earthly Kingdom of Jesus* (Los Angeles, CA: Theological Studies Press, 2015); Ron Rhodes, *The End Times in Chronological Order* (Eugene, OR: Harvest House, 2012); Paul Benware, *Understanding End Times Prophecy* (Chicago: Moody Press, 1995); and John MacArthur, *The Second Coming: Signs of Christ's Return and the End of the Age* (Wheaton, IL: Crossway Books, 2006).

7. John Wesley and Charles Wesley, *The Poetical Works of John and Charles Wesley*, ed. G. Osborn (London: Wesleyan-Methodist Conference Office, 1869), pp. 458-461.

CHAPTER 7—THERE IS NO HELL

1. Dante Alighieri, *The Divine Comedy*, Poetry in Translation, Kindle Edition, p. 17.

2. Alighieri, *The Divine Comedy*, p. 18.

3. Rob Bell, *Love Wins* (New York: HarperCollins, 2012), p. viii.

4. Satguru Sivaya Subramuniyaswami, *Dancing with Siva: Hinduism's Contemporary Catechism* (India: Himalayan Academy, 2003), p. 155.

5. *Dancing with Siva.*

6. B.C. Law, *Heaven and Hell in Buddhist Perspective* as quoted on "Buddhist Studies: Dharma Data: Hell," http://www.buddhanet.net/e-learning/dharmadata/fdd19.htm.

7. Mahasi Sayadaw, "The Theory of Karma," *Buddhist Studies*, http://www.buddhanet.net/e-learning /karma.htm.

8. Mary Baker Eddy, *Science and Health with Key to the Scriptures* (Boston: Christian Science Board of Directors), Kindle edition, locations 5118-5119.

9. Eddy, *Science and Health*, Kindle locations 3482-3483.

10. Ministerial Association of Seventh-Day Adventists, *Seventh-Day Adventists Believe…A Biblical Exposition of 27 Fundamental Doctrines* (Washington, DC: Review & Herald Publishing Association, 1988), p. 370.

11. "What Is Hell? Is It a Place of Eternal Torment?" *Jehovah Witnesses,* https://www.jw.org/en/ bible-teachings/questions/what-is-hell/.

12. See: F.F. Bruce's *The New Testament Documents: Are They Reliable?* (Grand Rapids, MI: Eerdmans, 1984); Gary Habermas's *The Historical Jesus: Ancient Evidence for the Life of Christ* (Joplin, MO: College Press, 1996); David Craig L. Blomberg's *The Historical Reliability of the Gospels* (Downers Grove, IL: InterVarsity, 1986); Michael J. Wilkins' *Jesus Under Fire* (Grand Rapids, MI: Zondervan, 1996); Phil Fernandez and Kyle Larson's *Hijacking the Historical Jesus: Answering Recent Attacks on the Jesus of the Bible* (Bremerton, WA: Institute of Biblical Defense, 2012); David Ewert's *From Ancient Tablets to Modern Translations: A General Introduction to the Bible* (Grand Rapids, MI: Zondervan, 1993; Norman Geisler and William Nix's *A General Introduction to the Bible* (Chicago: Moody Press, 1986); John MacArthur's *The Scripture Cannot Be Broken: Twentieth Century Writings on Inerrancy* (Wheaton, IL: Crossway, 2015); and Erwin W. Lutzer's *Seven Reasons Why You Can Trust the Bible* (Chicago: Moody Press, 1988).

13. W.G.T. Shedd, *Dogmatic Theology*, 3d ed. (Phillipsburg, NJ: P & R Publishing, 2003), p. 888.

14. C.W. Morgan and R.A. Peterson, eds., *Hell Under Fire: Modern Scholarship Reinvents Eternal Punishment* (Grand Rapids, MI: Zondervan, 2004), p. 240.

15. Brian D. McLaren, *The Story We Find Ourselves In: Further Adventures of a New Kind of Christian* (San Francisco, CA: Jossey-Bass, 2003), p. 102; Steve Chalke, *The Lost Message of Jesus* (Grand Rapids, MI: Zondervan, 2004), p. 182. In response to this perverse characterization to the substitutionary atonement of Christ, see D.A. Carson, T.R. Schreiner, B.A. Ware, and J. Hamilton, "The SBJT Forum: The Atonement under Fire," *Southern Baptist Journal of Theology*, vol. 11 (Summer 2007), pp. 96-114.

16. See Robert Peterson's *Hell on Trial: The Case for Eternal Punishment* (Phillipsburg, NJ: P & R Publishing, 1995); Christopher W. Morgan and Robert Peterson's *Hell Under Fire: Modern Scholarship Reinvents Eternal Punishment* (Grand Rapids, MI: Zondervan, 2004); Richard Mayhue, ed. *The Master's Seminary Journal*, vol. 9, no. 2 (Fall 1998), which includes five helpful essays on the doctrine of eternal punishment. Also see Ajith Fernando's *Crucial Questions About Hell* (Wheaton, IL:

Crossway, 1994) and Larry Dixon's *The Other Side of the Good News: Confronting the Challenges to Jesus' Teaching on Hell* (Ross-shire: Christian Focus, 2003).

17. R.A. Mohler Jr., "Modern Theology: The Disappearance of Hell" in Christopher W. Morgan and Robert Peterson, eds., *Hell Under Fire: Modern Scholarship Reinvents Eternal Punishment* (Grand Rapids, MI: Zondervan, 2004), p. 41.

CHAPTER 8—HELL'S GOING TO BE
ONE BIG PARTY WITH MY FRIENDS

1. Mark Twain, *The Complete Speeches by Mark Twain*, Kindle location 1148.

2. See "Twain Quote on Heaven" at http://www.twainquotes.com/Heaven.html, and also Mark Twain's "Captain Stormfield's Visit to Heaven" in *Five Short Novels* (CreateSpace Independent Publishing, 2014).

3. "Dead Man Talking," *The Guardian*, https://www.theguardian.com/world/2001/apr/22/mcveigh.usa.

4. D.J. Wieand, "Hinnom, Valley of" in *The International Standard Bible Encyclopedia*, vol. 2, ed. G.W. Bromiley (Grand Rapids, MI: Eerdmans, 1979–1988), p. 717.

5. L. Ryken, J. Wilhoit, T. Longman, C. Duriez, D. Penney, and D.G. Reid, in *Dictionary of Biblical Imagery*, elec. ed. (Downers Grove, IL: InterVarsity Press), p. 288.

6. Harry A. Ironside, *Addresses on the Gospel of Luke* (Neptune, NJ: Loizeaux Brothers, 1947), p. 516.

7. L. Ryken, J. Wilhoit, T. Longman, C. Duriez, D. Penney, and D.G. Reid, in *Dictionary of Biblical Imagery*, elec. ed. (Downers Grove, IL: InterVarsity Press), p. 377.

8. Jonathan Edwards, *The Works of Jonathan Edwards,* vol. 2 (Carlisle, PA: Banner of Truth Trust, 1974), pp. 9-12.

CHAPTER 9—HELL IS THE EXACT SAME
TERRIBLE EXPERIENCE FOR EVERYONE

1. Robert L. Thomas, *Revelation 8-22: An Exegetical Commentary* (Chicago: Moody Publishers, 1995) p. 431.

2. The only exception that can be argued is in the case of young children and those with severe mental impairment. For more on this see Robert Lightner's *Safe in the Arms of Jesus: God's Provision for the Death of Those Who Cannot Believe* (Grand Rapids, MI: Kregel, 2000); John MacArthur's *Safe in the Arms of God: Truth from Heaven about the Death of a Child* (Nashville, TN: Thomas Nelson, 2003); and Robert Alexander Webb's *Theology of Infant Salvation* (Barryville, VA: Hess Publishers, 1998).

3. See Millard J. Erickson's *How Shall They Be Saved? The Destiny of Those Who Do Not Hear of Jesus* (Baker Books, 1996); Paul House's *Who Will Be Saved? Defending the Biblical Understanding of God & Salvation* (Wheaton, IL: Crossway, 2000); Ronald Nash's *Is Jesus the Only Savior?* (Grand Rapids, MI: Zondervan, 1994); Richard Phillips, et al., *Only One Way? Reaffirming the Exclusive Truth Claims of Christianity* (Wheaton, IL: Crossway, 2007); and Ravi Zacharias's *Jesus Among Other Gods: The Absolute Claims of the Christian Message* (Nashville, TN: Word Publishing, 2000).

4. Larry Dixson, *The Other Side of the Good News: Confronting the Contemporary Challenges to Jesus's Teaching on Hell* (Wheaton, IL.: Victor Books, 1992), pp. 81-85.

5. Jonathan Edwards, *The Works of Jonathan Edwards,* vol. 2 (Carlisle, PA: Banner of Truth Trust, 1974), p. 10.

6. For several other biblical, linguistic, and theological reasons for an enduring penalty for earthly sins see Chris Morgan's *Jonathan Edwards & Hell* (Geanies House, Scotland: Christian Focus, 2004).

7. *Logos Hymnal,* 1st ed. (Oak Harbor, WA: Logos Research Systems, Inc., 1995).

CHAPTER 10—IT DOESN'T MATTER WHAT HAPPENS TO MY BODY AFTER I DIE

1. "Question Fourteen: Why Do Hindus Cremate the Dead?" *Hinduism Today*, http://www.hinduism today.com/modules/smartsection/item.php?itemid=5676.

2. L.A. Nichols, G.A. Mather, and A.J. Schmidt in *Encyclopedic Dictionary of Cults, Sects, and World Religions* (Grand Rapids, MI: Zondervan, 2006), p. 124. See also the article "Fire Worship" at https://en.wikipedia.org/wiki/Fire_worship (accessed August 18, 2017).

3. Saad Mohammed, director of Islamic Information for the Islamic Society of Greater Oklahoma City, cited in "Not a Dying Trend: This Is Why Cremations—and Religion—Keep Making Headlines in the U.S.," *Get Religion*, https://www.getreligion.org/getreligion/2017/8/15/not-a-dying-trend-this-is-why-cremations-and-religion-keep-making-headlines-in-the-us.

4. "Jewish Views on Cremation" at *My Jewish Learning,* http://www.myjewishlearning.com/article/judaism-on-cremation/.

5. "2016 NFDA Cremation and Burial Report Released: Rate of Cremation Surpasses That of Burial in 2015," National Funeral Directors Association, http://www.nfda.org/news/media-center/nfda-news-releases/id/1310/2016-nfda-cremation-and-burial-report-released-rate-of-cremation-surpasses-that-of-burial-in-2015.

6. "In a Move Away from Tradition, Cremations Increase," *The New York Times*, https://www .nytimes.com/2017/08/10/nyregion/cremations-increase-in-a-move-away-from-tradition.html.

7. "Instruction Ad Resurgendum cum Christo regarding the burial of the deceased and the conservation of the ashes in the case of cremation, 25.10.2016," Holy See Press Office, http://press.vatican.va/content/salastampa/en/bollettino/pubblico/2016/10/25/161025c.html.

8. See Fred Rosen's *Cremation in America* (New York: Prometheus Books, 2004) and Steven Prothero's *Purified by Fire: A History of Cremation in America* (Berkeley, CA: University of California Press, 2001).

9. D.N. Freedman, ed., "Burials" in *The Anchor Yale Bible Dictionary*, vol. 1 (New York: Doubleday, 1992), p. 785.

10. G.S. Ogden and L. Zogbo, *A Handbook on Ecclesiastes* (New York: United Bible Societies, 1998), p. 196; M.A. Eaton, *Ecclesiastes: An Introduction and Commentary*, vol. 18 (Downers Grove, IL: InterVarsity Press, 1983), p. 121.

11. Albert Mohler, "The Briefing," August 15, 2017, http://www.albertmohler.com/2017/08/15/briefing-08-15-17/.

12. Got Questions Ministries, *Got Questions? Bible Questions Answered* (Bellingham, WA: Logos Bible Software, 2002–2013).

13. "Christian Death: Mourn or Celebrate," *The Gospel Coalition*, https://blogs.thegospelcoalition.org/kevindeyoung/2014/05/29/christian-death-mourn-or-celebrate/; "Funeral, Not a 'Celebration of Life'" *Breakpoint*, http://www.breakpoint.org/2017/07/the-point-funeral-not-celebration-of-life/; "Don't Force the Celebration at Funerals" *Christianity Today*, http://www.christianitytoday.com/ct/2016/march/dont-force-celebration-at-funerals.html; and "I Don't Want a Celebration of Life, I Want a Burial Service," *Anglican Pastor*, http://anglicanpastor.com/i-dont-want-a-celebration-of-life-i-want-a-burial-service/.

ALSO BY MIKE FABAREZ

Lifelines for Tough Times

When hard times hit, we often find ourselves vulnerable—to doubt, fear, worry, even depression. We ask, "Does God care? Has He forgotten me?"

So why does God allow suffering? Author Mike Fabarez—who is well acquainted with deep pain himself as the father of a special-needs child and as a pastor who has counseled many through life's hurts—looks to the truths of Scripture for answers. Along the way, he shares...

- how complete trust in God alone can restore your confidence and hope
- the power of focusing on God's eternal goals for you in life's temporary setbacks
- God's promise to love and protect you no matter what happens

This book will not only help you to understand why God allows suffering—it will provide you with the resources to stand strong, rest in God's care, and endure!

To learn more about Harvest House books and
to read sample chapters, visit our website:

www.harvesthousepublishers.com

HARVEST HOUSE PUBLISHERS
EUGENE, OREGON